THE MAKING
OF A
SECOND WORLD NATION

Parents and Educators Are Causing
THE MAKING OF A SECOND WORLD NATION

Joyce Gardner Wagner

Eloquent Books
Durham, Connecticut

Eloquent Books
An imprint of Strategic Book Group
P. O. Box 333
Durham, CT 06422
http://www.strategicbookgroup.com

ISBN: 978-1-60976-205-6

Book Design by Julius Kiskis

Dedication

To all living and future children of my children

With loving hope that they will be encouraged and gently urged

At home and at school

To become

The best they can be.

Human History

Becomes More And More

A Race Between

Education And Castastrophe

H. G. WELLS

Contents

INTRODUCTION

I wrote this book twenty years ago. Recently, I decided to up-date and re-write it. In these past twenty years, nothing has changed in scholastic abilities of American school students. The sad truth is that the problems existing in schools and in homes twenty years ago, still exist today. If anything, it has gotten worse. With all the latest talk of our failed educational system, nothing constructive and beneficial has taken place to change the situation.

Then and now, there has been much concern over apparent failure of American schools to effectively educate our nation's youth. For the past fifty years, public teaching institutions have been inundated with what experts in the field have coined "new and innovative ideas which have failed to promote positive scholastic results. Although this incessant experimentation has been manifested in Johnny's inability to read or to learn, not one thought has been given to methods of yester-year when Johnny could read and learn well. A search for what educators have perceived as practical education to work in conjunction with changing times has resulted in confusion and ineptness on the part of parents, teachers, and ultimately our American students.

I taught in the public schools fifty yeas ago, and have taught in the elementary and high schools in recent years. I have seen first-hand which methods of teaching result in effective learning, and which do not. I have witnessed changes in parenting and classroom decorum on the part of teachers and students.

Newspaper headlines still scream international statistics such as a 2008 article in the WASHINGTON POST stating "U.S. STUDENTS' SCIENCE TEST PERFORMANCE STAGNATES". A January, 2008 report by the National Council on Teacher Quality states that most states receive low marks, that of C- and lower. The study was based on the ability to identify effective teachers; retaining effective teachers, and dismissing ineffective teachers.

The bibliography at the end of this book is filled with sources obtained twenty years ago. I've kept them there for a purpose. The statistics have not altered much! The irony here is that educational failures have remained throughout our elementary and high schools and even our colleges and universities since I first took pen to paper to disclose such facts. Yet parents and teachers alike want children to learn and succeed. Today, everyone wants things to happen for the good, only they are not willing to make changes that produce the kinds of effort necessary in the production of excellent results.

A good friend of mine opined that this is an excellent manuscript, and one that says what is needed to be said, but stated," You attack teachers and parents alike. Everyone will be mad at you." This is true! I hope, however, that in the midst of their ire, they will recognize the truth within these pages, and respond and react according to these truths. One can only hope!

My experiences vary greatly as a teacher. You will read about them as you progress within these pages. As I have amassed knowledge from my experiences, I have been astounded at the lack of parental and school discipline. For five years before retiring permanently, I taught in a school for learning-disabled children, grades one through high school. It was a small, expensive, private school, and for some of the children, their last hope. Although most of the children possessed impediments of various kinds pertaining to learning capabilities, many of them suffered from another problem, which led to difficulties in learning and retaining information. That problem was LOW EXPECTATIONS on the part of parents and teachers. I was appalled at the lack of discipline throughout the entire school. Children who possessed behavioral problems and emotional problems were acquiesced to on a regular basis. Our principal repeatedly made statements such as, "You know, we have to cut them some slack because they have problems with self discipline." And I repeatedly asked,"How in the world are they going to overcome and master their problems if they are allowed to nurture them?"

After having taught in the school for six months or more, parents and teachers, alike, were dubbing me "the miracle teacher", because my students were actually learning. I taught ages six through eleven years. One seven-year-old girl was quite delayed mentally, and could not read nor print, so I concentrated on those skills first. I took her letter-by-letter to help her to read, and letter by letter to help her to print. She needed to work on small and large motor skills over and over and over. At the end of a month's time, she could read simple words, knew all the sounds of the alphabet, and could print beautifully, making perfect lettering with "driveways" between each word, etc. The point is, I didn't settle for less, and together we practiced until her reading skills, and her printing skills were the best she could do, which as it turned out, were very, very good. Her parents could hardly believe her improved skills, and that little girl was thrilled with her accomplishments.

I had a ten year old boy in my class who could not stay in his seat for more than a few minutes at a time, could not read because he was too hyper to focus his eyes on the page for more than a few seconds, and was a behavior problem beyond description. Before he could be expected to attend to anything, including seatwork, he had to learn to discipline himself, and he had to learn to read. To teach him how to read, I sat beside him and first put my arm around him to let him know that I was on his side, and not against him, and also to "steady" him physically. I then explained to him what we were going to do. Then I taught him to read by putting my hands on each side of his head, creating "blinders" such as one sees on a horse. That boy learned to read one word at a time.

Because I expected each student to quietly attend to his or her seatwork, finish it, then check for mistakes before handing in their finished product, I needed to let this young lad know that the same was expected of him. To expect him to stay in his seat long enough to finish even one paper was totally unrealistic, so I gave him the entire paper, then drew a line about a fourth of the way down, and informed him that he must finish just that much. Of course he was not able to do so at one time, without getting up to move about, so I told the principal that she was going to receive several "important" envelopes throughout the day from me, and there was not going to be a damn thing in them but a blank sheet of paper. Thus, this young fellow worked for a few minutes on his seatwork, whereby I would ask him to please deliver an important message to the principal. This accomplished two things; he was able to get out of his seat while still obeying the classroom rules, and he was given a sense of importance, which he so lacked.

Before the first report card marking period, that young boy was able to read three pre-primers, and had begun his first hardcover book. I no longer had to hold my hands beside his eyes. He was able to stay in his seat and concentrate on his work for at least twenty minutes, and complete a couple of pages. By the end of the year, he had begun a fourth grade book, which meant that he was nearly up to grade level.

The public school system in which he had been enrolled, had given up on him, and had told his (divorced) parents that there was nothing more they could do for him. I had been a last hope for that boy. His birth father had also given up on him, and rarely saw him, which broke this kid's heart. Before I knew it, there were requests from his former school district to monitor my class, and observe my teaching. They did not believe their eyes when they observed his behavior and his academic accomplishments. They returned a couple of times, not having fully believed, at first, what they had witnessed. (They also offered me a job) Upon their queries as to how I performed this "miracle", I answered, "Diligence and high expectations and lots of patience!" I never held the thought that something is "good enough." I have always, when teaching children, aimed for the very best they could be.

It filled my heart with pure joy, when my principal came into my classroom after Christmas vacation, and announced, "You will never guess who just called the school. She had tears in her eyes when she told me, "It was -----'s father, who was weeping on the phone when he stated, 'I have my boy back! He can read and write, and we actually had a great time together, because he has turned into a pretty nice kid to be with." I, too, wept upon hearing this, and said, "Now a boy has his father back." It was days like that that make me miss teaching today.

Yet it was not always easy to stick to my guns. I always used behavior modification when I taught, a system of classroom management. The children received stars when they accomplished good things, behaviorally and academically. Sometimes I had to be unusually alert to find the good, but it was vitally important that I did so, and most of the time there was something good to find. They received zeros for poor behavior, both behaviorally and academically, such as purposefully handing in sloppy work so they could have "free time", or not finishing work, etc. I would always explain to them why their behavior was good or bad and why they received stars or zeros. This system gives children immediate feedback, which is important, especially with young children. I gave each student their own personally designed behavior report paper at the end of each day to take home for his or her parents to sign. The next morning I would collect their behavior report papers, signed by parents and I would file them. (If a paper was not signed, the parent would get a phone call from me) At the end of the week, I added up all the stars, subtracted the zeros, and the amount of stars left would then be turned into pretend money with which they would purchase items from our school store. They even had their own checkbooks, which they balanced as part of math class. They learned how to write checks to purchase goods. If they could not afford a particular item they wished to buy, they could put it on "lay-away", and save up for it. Talk about motivation to behave well and produce acceptable work!

With the behavior modification system in classroom management, it is vitally important to be consistent. Many teachers will let a situation slide often for reasons of convenience, thereby lowering the expectations of the children. My personal motto was to praise the good throughout the entire day, often in front of the rest of the students, revealing to them what IS good behavior, and to chastise poor behavior privately with the student. Children will soon learn good from bad, and will know that they are respected.

The five years I taught in that small school were some of the most rewarding years of my career. Several teachers from other school districts came to observe my teaching methods, and were astounded at how quiet and orderly the classroom was, yet how loud and fun it was during playtime. A T.V. channel in our city did a documentary on "Women Who Make a Difference", and when several parents told them about me, they came with cameras flashing. The most joy I felt, though, was when parents, with tears in their eyes, told me that I not only changed the life of their child, but I changed the dynamics of their entire family.

Excellent teaching can take place in today's world if a teacher is brave enough to try. There will always be one or two parents who insist that their child should not have to work hard to do well in school. Gifted children who make that opinion true are few and far between, but unfortunately the numbers of parents who express this nonsense are growing in leaps and bounds.

Education is necessary for any country to become and remain a first world nation. The great, ancient philosophers evidenced a profound belief in the infinite benefits of preeminent education. Indeed, throughout the centuries of mankind's socialization, great men have recognized the basic need for citizenry knowledge in order for a society to thrive and evolve into something better. We all travel through life thirsting for mental growth. Evidence from recent studies has indicated that this desire for intelligence begins with the unborn child as he constantly and actively seeks new, ongoing knowledge from his darkened womb. Unborn children have been known to learn to find their thumbs to suck. They cry when in an uncomfortable position. Many have music preferences. Hard rock music, for example, often agitates an unborn child, while symphonic music soothes and relaxes. All of this is knowledge sought and grasped by tiny beings, not yet born into our world.

Think then, about the wonders learned throughout the ages, from the invention of fire and spears, to discoveries in outer space by revolving satellites. Learning is an ongoing, eternal thing--- an earthly infinity. It is a natural phenomenon of mankind, and will continue to be so until the demise of the universe. Such a natural propensity should be allowed and encourage to grow, and thrive, and improve within each century, each decade, each day, and the most productive way to do this is through the process of formal education for all of our citizens.

Ancient Greece was perhaps among the first of civilized cultures to promote a liberal education program for its people, with the fundamental philosophy that in doing so, the society of Athens itself would excel. Rome followed suit to a lesser degree, and since those ancient times a multitude of cultures have adopted the tenet that education is important, not only for the good of the individual, but also for the good of society.

The folks of the new and exciting country called America were of this opinion two hundred years ago. They instituted a policy of free education for all, and then went so far as to make it mandatory. Actually, the educational system of the United States of America was one of our first welfare programs; indeed, the only welfare program to really work, for it is designed to cause in people, INDEPENDENCE, not DEPENDENCE. American education was also designed to ensure that no one should be excluded.

Yet today, when one mentions the general condition of our nation's educational system, he sparks a fire of controversy, anger, and frustration over the manner in which America children are taught. That anger and frustration is justified! But it is not only the schools that are failing the American people. It is the American people who have failed themselves! Of every thousand women in the United States, forty-three are unwed mothers, and the ratio is growing. It has become a status symbol today, for teenaged girls to have a baby. It is universally accepted for unmarried men and women to live together, and "R" rated movies are consistent box office hits. Television programs continue to be flooded with sex and violence to such an extent that many of us have become desensitized to vulgar speech, sexual innuendos, and grisly crimes. Even seemingly innocent movies are sure to have those one or two vulgarities so they can be termed PG13, and therefore attract audiences. Why?

What has transpired between the founding of our country and now? What exactly has taken place in school classrooms and in American homes over the past century? Approximately when did we begin to read articles on "Why Johnny can't read", and how long did it take us to realize those articles were written because Johnny CAN'T read? Who and what caused the decline in scholastic and moral performance of America's youth, and what can be done to rectify the situation?

This book is not meant to focus primarily on in-depth

methodology of teaching. Its purpose is to investigate and bring to light the developments that have taken place in American schools and homes, and to address the various causes of a decided breakdown in classroom effectiveness. It offers creative solutions to our vast problems for both the home and the school, with a sincere hope for the positive future of our great nation.

Part I

HISTORY OF AMERICAN SCHOOLS

When free public education began, it was founded on the principle that in order for our young nation to accomplish the monumental aspirations of its people, it needed its future adults to be learned individuals. This was, at the time, not a wholly popular idea. Nearly ninety percent of early Americans were hard working farmers who depended on the entire family for physical support on the homestead, and deemed it excessively inconvenient to sacrifice family manpower. As small farms grew into larger ones, there became an even more urgent need for sons, especially, to remain at home to tend to vast agricultural demands. Needless to say, our nation's first schools, especially in the countryside, were crude, small, and housed very few students.

Public education was met with higher approval in our first towns and cities. The populace here consisted mainly of small shop owners and their employees, along with tradesmen and artisans, and those involved in the shipping industry. There was a more distinct separation if social classes in the city, which, for a time, influenced student enrollment. The wealthy businessmen and landowners did not require the physical or financial support of their children for survival, thus these children were able to attend school regularly. There were, on the other hand, many citizens of early America who needed the income of every family member in order to exist in even substandard fashion. Added to this crisis of the urban poor, was the eventual influx of "huddled masses" from nations of other parts of the world, causing employment shortages throughout most of our Eastern and some mid-Western states. Although most of the cities' poor yearned for their children to be educated, it appeared impossible, for it was considered sheer lunacy to sacrifice family members to several hours at school when they were so sorely needed to add to the family income.

As cities grew, and jobs became scarce, employee abuse, even of young children, became wide- spread. It became increasingly evident that in this new land of freedom, steps should be taken to ensure that ALL children should receive a free education. Social reformers set out to publicize and correct the deplorable situation children faced in factories and warehouses during the industrial revolution, which eventually led to the decision that public education should be mandatory.

This gradual procedure was characterized by a multitude of phases. In both the farmlands and in the cities, it was reasoned that only boys were in need of a formal education; young girls did not require such intellect to prepare for roles as wives and mothers, and usually remained at home to learn domestic skills. As a larger number of schools were installed across the nation, and social and political pressures were brought to bear, daughters were gradually included in school enrollments. Soon, primary schools sprang up, seemingly overnight, and secondary schools were eventually erected. Schools to teach teachers were instituted, and finally a full-scale public education system was begun.

Much has taken place since that time. The democratic principles and public school management have grown slowly through process of trial and error. Urban schools have been responsible to electoral votes for more than one hundred years. For much of that time, however, the preponderant force was upper-middle-class business and community leaders who often combined to moderate the efforts of immigrant groups to control schools. The elite feared that such lower class influence would open the schools to patronage and distant educational programs for political, ethnic, and anti-intellectual purposes. These groups characterized themselves as reformers and progressives. [1]

In most ways, this tide of thinking has changed throughout the electoral vote, but the functions of American Schools, and many parents' attitudes toward education, have made this early fear of "dumbing down" of school aspirations a grim reality. The American declaration that we are all created equal in the sense that each person is born with equal worth as an esteemed individual has always played a major role in our nation's system of education. While it is a fact of life that we are not equally endowed by beauty, intelligence, physical or emotional skills, an emphasis on equality in education has rightfully, throughout this century and the past century, taken precedence in school priorities. Within reasonable guidelines of respectful and prudent behavioral standards for mankind's best interest, each human being is entitled to life, liberty, and to pursue happiness. Education is probably the most powerful tool with which to procure these forms of freedom successfully. In accordance with this philosophy, all American grade schools, high schools, colleges and universities have historically aspired to be spawning grounds for future generations of elites.

The fact is, most places of learning were exceedingly effective well into the twentieth century. Teachers chose to be teachers because they believed it to be their vocation. Most educators delighted in enriching the minds of youth, and although they did not always employ the best methods, especially in regard to effective classroom management, I believe they taught with what they perceived as best methods. Most of us are relieved that the day of the painful and demeaning hickory stick has passed, but in truth, extensive learning did take place in conjunction with that oft-time form of discipline, as evidenced by the 1895 eighth grade final exam included in the back of this book.

Those who employed that hickory stick did not face an easy life in those early times. Obligations and duties that seem ludicrous today were taken for granted in schools of yester-year. Water barrels needed to be installed in classrooms, coal hauled in, furnaces fired up, windows, floors, and chalkboards required constant upkeep. The teacher's schoolroom was her domain, and while she exercised her responsibilities to oversee these many functions, something took place in school that is no longer in evidence in our modern day schools. There was an overwhelming pride in the school, as each member took an active interest in its maintenance. Since many chores had to be done, it was necessary for everyone involved, teachers and students, to participate in carrying out these duties, precipitating a feeling of pride and unity. Learning was an honored privilege, not to be taken lightly.

Children were taught to respect ALL adults, including, but not exclusive to, parents and teachers. (Some teachers up to and including the early years of the twentieth century, were very young) This respect carried over into the classroom, and although a teacher may have had discipline problems in dealing with mischievous demonstrations between students, she rarely was faced with disrespect toward her. This prevailing deference to authority was paramount to maintaining order in the classrooms, because although many private institutions were staffed with male teachers, most public schools were taught by women, and in many cases, young girls not much older than their students.

As school enrollments grew, newer school buildings arose. These schools consisted of several classrooms, which segregated students into specific age groups. Life in educational institutions became more complex with the installation of electricity, central heating, and with use of pencils and paper to replace slate boards. Daily demands of the teacher changed with the times. She no longer was required to oversee the rudimentary tasks of the antiquated schoolroom; no water buckets, no furnace to fire, no candles to preserve. She was now in charge of the bathroom brigade, and the recess playground, not to mention her after-school duties at teachers' meetings. She was also better educated, having attended her state's teachers' college, and although she was still not paid well, she was offered better financial benefits than ever before. In spite of all this, she soon came to resent having to extend her professional duties to that of bathroom sentry and playground overseer. She also reasoned that she was paid too little in view of her years of scholarly preparation. Women, and now men, began to see teaching as a profession, rather than as an underpaid vocation. Ergo - The teachers' unions.

But what was happening behind the scenes at this time? Several factors came into play, which caused the basic philosophy of American education to change. The economic prosperity of the roaring twenties caused social and philosophical thinking to change from a work ethic mentality to a euphoric, pleasure-seeking system of beliefs. Prohibition, designed to suppress unrestrained social behavior, generated a culture of speak-easies, bathtub gin, and a sort of early century sexual revolution. Although respect for authority still prevailed within the lives of children, city parents and young adults were having the time of their lives. It was an era of financial and emotional release after the First World War, and celebration in a country that had spent the last one hundred years striving for such a respite.

Several beneficial aspects accompanied this new economic boon. Aesthetic appreciation of the cultural arts livened the mind and spirit in cities all across the nation. Although the still-struggling Midwest farmers experienced very little of this revelry, folks in American cities enjoyed more money and more leisure time than they ever had before. Unions had already become a reality, especially in the North, and people had funds and the time to patronize the arts. The entertainment business grew as a result of both philosophy and lifestyles, and creative juices flowed during this post WW1 period of peace and prosperity.

But while this air of carefree abandonment reigned in America, international events were taking place that would alter our country's educational system forever. The aftermath of WW1 resulted in Europe's powerful, huge empires being broken into small, politically and militarily ineffective nations. Russia, engrossed in her Bolshevik Revolution during the war, had now embraced Marx and Engel's MANIFESTO with full zeal.

The Bolshevik Revolution eventually found Stalin, and Communism reared its ugly head. Given that European countries no longer held the power they once enjoyed, it was only a matter of time after WW11, for Stalin to take advantage of America's willingness to divide Berlin. Marx and Engel's dream of conquering Europe by force had come to fruition. America, however, required a different approach, and Leningrad set out to facilitate the necessary measures with which to influence American thinking. Marx had reasoned that if mass discontent and turmoil were to take place in America, Communism would appear as the saving ideology, thereby procuring the conversion of the United States from within America itself. The Soviet plan was to infiltrate from the bottom up (America's factories) and from the top down (America's teaching colleges and universities). The manifestation of this plan had already taken place in our factories. Socialists here had taken full advantage of the injustices leveled at factory and warehouse workers, and the idea of our country as a Republic gave way to a new ideology of absolute Democracy. Individuals demanded individual recognition and respect. This situation created ease in the employment of half-truth propaganda on the part of "planted" Soviet sympathizing workers. Folks love to hear that they will be given something for free that they do not necessarily have to work very hard for.

From the "top", Communists infiltrated numerous major colleges and universities across the United States. In the late nineteen forties and throughout the fifties, it was not unusual for there to be several "card-carrying" Communist professors teaching at the college level, many of whom were schooled in Russia before being strategically installed in American learning institutions. Although they taught in diversified areas, the majority of these Communist professors taught political science. They also taught many subjects to prospective elementary and high school teachers. They seized the opportunity to influence young, vulnerable minds by presenting to them a brave new philosophy, with the suggestion that these young intellects break away from parental archaic thinking. The idea, of course, was to have a snowball effect on future America. Ingrain those who would go out into primary and secondary schools, who, in turn, would ingrain socialistic credos into the minds of the very young. We are used to hearing the news media discuss with abhorrence, "the dreaded McCarthy era." True, there were examples of wanton disregard for citizen rights of privacy, but what we rarely, if ever hear today is the vast number of Communists these investigations unearthed; folks who were dedicated to the destruction of American democracy. As a co-ed at Michigan State University in the middle and late fifties, I had no less than a dozen professors who espoused socialism and Communism in their classrooms and lecture theatres. Those profs did their jobs well and effectively, for today, it is rare to find a college or university professor who is NOT a socialist. Khrushchev, when visiting the United States, declared that Communism would rule in America, in the lives of our granddaughters and grandsons. He said this in the fifties. In 2009, America elected a president who wants to "redistribute" the wealth of its citizens. "FROM each, according to their abilities, TO each according to their needs" sounds frighteningly similar.

The small town in which I attended high school had such a teacher; an excellent teacher of English and literature, who admitted to belonging to a "card-carrying" Communist group at Michigan State University. While we were learning skills to evaluate published magazines and newspapers, he ordered 'THE DAILY WORKER' as one of the various materials we were to critique. He was very subtle in his support of Communist ethos, and we agreed with everything he said to us. He was a young man who related well to high school students, and we were young, growing minds, eager to break away from parental psychological ties to form what we perceived to be our "own" opinions. We also felt a sense of security with this teacher. After all, he was an adult and an adult such as he would not lead us far astray. We had no idea he was manipulating our minds, and when finally he was asked to leave the school system, we were positively incensed! How could such a narrow- minded administration do such a terrible thing to such a wonderful man? Yet, if he were teaching today, I fear the administrative school body would not only keep him in the system, but would agree with his principles. Why? Because most of today's school administrators and teachers are products of Marx's plan installed at the "top".

Employing such teachers is an extremely effective way in which to promote radical thinking in the minds of young, pliable students, to turn the tide of political thinking in future voters, to stem a student's ability to reason effectively and realistically, and ultimately to render a nation powerless in terms of social strength and technological advancement. There is no doubt in my mind that the past nefarious Soviet efforts in the United States, in factory unions and in schools, have played a major role in the demise of the American family unit, and in the lessening of classroom discipline and learning in our schools.

Some educators state that there were other reasons American education changed drastically throughout the nineteen fifties, although those reasons are not clear, since no rationales are given. It is only clear that the natural process of children's growth, changed from order to chaos.

The emergence of the Eisenhower years brought a feeling of peace and prosperity once more to our nation. We had healed from the GREAT DEPRESSION and WW11, and in spite of the Korean Conflict, there seemed to be a resurgence of unrestrained optimism. An atmosphere of carefree abandonment transpired with the introduction of Elvis, Rock and Roll, the Beatles, and Dr. Spock. Never before had generations so blatantly veered from parental approval and traditional principles at so young an age. Self –discipline was de-emphasized in favor of self-expression. Now, for the first time since the turn of the century, Freud was embraced, then scrutinized, then evaluated. Dr. Spock's book on child- care caused the entire nation to fall into a sort of cult society in regard to permissive behavior.

In the sixties, educators sought what they considered to be practical education to work in conjunction with the changing times. This was a period of confusion, for psychologists themselves, were attempting to re-define mental and emotional health. This movement really began in the middle fifties, and grew to huge proportions through the sixties. As a student in the college of education, I was taught to encourage first graders to color elephants purple, instead of grey. This, I as told, encouraged creativity on the part of such students. This reasoning didn't make sense to me then, and it does not make sense to me now. The terms "creativity" and "reality" tended to switch around and round and often interpretations were identified at the whim of each educator. Realistically, an elephant is grey. If a child WANTED to paint a purple elephant, it would perhaps indicate that he was creatively branching out to a higher level of aesthetic sensibilities. But to actually tell a small child to color an elephant purple is to confuse the issues of reality. Being well aware that creativity and reality enhance each other, for some reason educators traveled to opposing poles to make the connection, thereby clouding the issues completely.

Attached to the debate of creativity vs. reality was the adoption of the pleasure theory. It was decided that a child could not learn effectively if he did not enjoy all the aspects and procedures it took to learn. John Silbur wrote in STRAIGHT SHOOTING: WHAT' WRONG WITH AMERICA AND HOW TO FIX IT: "Too often we put the pursuit of pleasure before the pursuit of happiness" He stated that children grow up today without learning to understand what he calls "the reality principle"; the need to face certain inevitable facts and limitations of life, and teaching them to confront these realities is a responsibility that modern parents and educators, unlike those of past generations, have shirked. "It never crossed the minds of eighteenth and nineteenth century parents or teachers that their principle responsibility was to be a pal to their children, or to try to make life easy, comfortable, convenient, or maximally pleasurable for them." [3] Silbur points out the damage we can do to children if this thought and behavior persists to a great degree.

Let's take a look at the suicide rate of adolescents and teenagers over the past forty years. Prior to the 1960's, young people were not told that they could expect life to be a bed of roses every day of the year. Life is a constant struggle, and we knew it! We knew from the time we were very young, that whether one was rich or poor, beautiful or plain, mentally astute or not, nothing came free from effort, nor did life come free from strife. Good days and bad were the diet of living, and we were taught to analyze, cope, solve if possible, and move forward. Today, young people are not emotionally prepared to deal with ordinary, everyday facts of life. They've been told by examples of parents, teachers, movie idols, T.V. shows, newspapers, and every other communication force that they have every right to expect their each and every day to be problem free. They are not told that sometimes challenges give renewed meaning to life, and overcoming obstacles is often self-validating. No wonder so many kids kill themselves when they meet an over-abundance of bad luck. They have been told over and over that life should always be fair and easy for them, and if it isn't, then life has no value, or it is the fault of someone else. To their mind, the act of committing suicide is merely destroying something that wasn't that valuable anyway. How terribly sad!

Good education not only is a necessary prerequisite for good job performance, (which seems to be the focus of recent laments about the future of our schools), but first and foremost as a basis of self-knowledge. Great works of literature should be read because they are about us, about our humanity; they're a distillation of human experience, good and ill.

Parents and especially educators of the sixties lost sight of this wisdom. They theorized that pleasure and enjoyment were necessary ingredients to offer school children. Thus appeared the open classroom. The open classroom, espoused its proponents, was designed to promote creative thinking in each individual child in accordance with his unique abilities. The belief of a norm for a child's development was completely discarded. His interests, enjoyment, and personal pleasures were thought to be the major components by which he would learn best. In other words, there was no longer a fourth grade skills development and ability, and it was considered perfectly normal for a fourth grader to progress at the level of an early third grader or a sixth grader. The fourth grade teacher was to recognize this and teach EACH child in her class according to his unique style and skills development and interests. There was, therefore, no structure of learning within the classroom environment. How could there be? The so-called experts failed to realize that good teachers of yester-year often recognized unique abilities of students, and gave these persons the extra attention and instruction needed to cater to the students' best interest. But in the sixties, it was thought to be a progressive and innovative breakthrough in the field of education to push this successful method of teaching to the extreme. As in the case of many extreme measures, a few vital factors were missing, having been thrown out by so-called modern thinkers.

First of all, in order for each child to have been given individual incentive, attention, instruction, and evaluation, there really was a need for more than one teacher per classroom. One teacher cannot effectively give thirty different children thirty different instructions requiring thirty different lesson plans, and design thirty unique means of evaluation testing. I know! When I taught in the private school for learning-disabled children, I had but eight students in my class at any given time, and I most often needed to design eight unique lessons to accommodate the needs of each child. It was not an easy task to do this on a daily basis. Imagine a regular classroom of thirty or so students. Impossible! Also, remember that this was the beginning of the "me" generation, when it was considered proper behavior for each child to demand constant, individual attention.

Students lacked the incentive to excel within this atmosphere because children were allowed to progress at their comfortable pace level. Thus, there was no desire on the part of the student to get from point A to point B. There was no measuring device to determine whether a child was performing at ability level, and contrary to the experts' thinking, there are adequate guidelines within an area deemed "norm" in behavioral and scholastic performance abilities of specific age groupings. A good teacher has historically done everything in her power to cater to individual talents, problems, and needs of her students, but this should always be carried out within certain degrees of limitations. This is not to say that a fourth grader who is performing at third grade level will never catch up, especially if he is given extra help to do so. Children often develop at various states of maturity. Even if this child reaches sixth grade, and still is progressing at a slower level than his classmates, a dedicated teacher must offer extra encouragement and aid. While no teacher should ignore individual needs of each classroom student, emphasis must still be put on the grade she is teaching. For instance, a fourth grade teacher concentrates heavily on fourth grade subject matter and learning skills, while giving extra help to those who are performing at third grade level, and offering extra challenges to those who are functioning at a fifth grade level.

This commonsense approach was not applied in the open classroom. While I was no longer teaching at the height of this open classroom mania, having elected to stay home to care for my children, I was none the less, deeply involved in public schools as a parent. (Fortunately, my children soon enrolled in a parochial school,) As a volunteer mother, I spent many days throughout each month in these disorderly environments, and witnessed first hand their total chaos. Often, since there were no walls between rooms, the distraction level was intense, not merely for the students, but for the teacher, as well. It really didn't matter, though, because nothing much was actually taught, anyway, and even less was learned. Children constantly roamed around the room, sharpening pencils, chatting with fellow classmates, or playing games. Yes, games were, and are today, integral facets in classrooms décor, considered healthy outlets and tools to generate learning pleasure. Games, then and now were not utilized exclusively for recess and bad weather days. Since the inception of the open classroom, they have been used as normal classroom activity, even in the upper elementary grades.

A DETROIT NEWS editorial sums up the situation exquisitely. It states that educators "peddled their progressive wares to gullible school systems that swallowed such elixirs as open classrooms, open space, social promotions, values clarifications, the new math, and other curriculum abominations. Academic standards were sacrificed, grades inflated, dress codes scrapped, and due process replaced discipline. Consequently, schools have regressed from playpens to pigpens, and finally into combat zones where neither staff nor students are safe. Simply stated, the lunatics are running the asylum. Critics, who complain that public schools have gone berserk, are dismissed as reactionaries, and anxious parents are advised to leave their children's education to the "experts". (4)

What were the results of this progressive education? It gradually became evident that children were not reading at grade level, and math proficiency had declined at a rapid rate. National and state science fair awards resembled a list of "who's who" in parochial schools, which, by the way, operated on very little money. Sagging standard test scores were blamed on the tests. It was, in fact, the birth of functional illiteracy that has grown to such proportions, that today, colleges need to offer courses in remedial reading, math, and spelling, and businesses spend a great deal of time and money training their people how to write an intelligent letter.

The early eighties found educators devising new ways of learning, and new methods of teaching. The results of the sixties and seventies proved to be embarrassing, but of course no one was prepared to admit that mistakes had been made. Instead of reevaluating former methods which had been discarded in the fifties, they raced impetuously onward to what they termed new and exciting avenues. The trouble, said the experts, was that children did not experience ENOUGH enjoyment while learning. Children would excel only if they found MORE pleasure in school. So it was proposed to prospective teachers in colleges and universities across the nation that a high interest approach to teaching was just the thing to work.

Again, these education pros managed to embrace a true concept and bastardize it to the point that the "baby was thrown out with the bathwater". The result was that, for awhile, children did have more fun in school; in fact, that is what they did best. But while all this fun was taking place, classroom discipline was declining proportionally, since the new philosophy of education was that children should be allowed to behave in any manner that caused them to feel good. This unrestricted behavior of students was deemed to be emotionally healthy, and teachers were actually evaluated on how much enjoyment was going on in her classroom, not on how much her students were learning.

Parents didn't help much here, either. Many a teacher became unpopular with parents because he or she required too much homework, or refused to inflate grades for poor performances. A really dedicated teacher, aware of true and vital exercises necessary to adequate learning, did not stand a chance in the midst of this "neo-pop" teaching culture.

This type of reasoning has continued throughout recent years, and has caused schoolrooms and school children to be at emotional and physical risk. It must be recognized that freedom to display unrestricted behavior results in a correlated lack of discipline, which, in turn causes a lack of freedom from harm. Unless you are a pretty tough survivor, not only on the recess playground, but in the classroom as well, you feel the pinch of such "freedom for all". At a time when teachers are supposedly most aware of the emotional desires of their students, the physical and emotional threats to many school children are overwhelming. Within the context of this classroom song of freedom, a macabre movement has developed. The belief in the good of free expression, no matter how crude that expression may be, has often resulted in the classroom aggressor being given a higher priority than victims of such aggression. Schools, today, have become unsafe places in which to dwell.

This liberal philosophical belief in the benefits of allowing unsuppressed, injudicious behavior in children has taken place in America's homes, as well as in her schools. Since the commencement of the nineteen sixties, home life has evolved from that of parent structured to child dominated environments. Dr. Spock was widely read, and parents all over our nation came to believe that if it is best to spare the rod, then it is good to spoil the child. I do not believe in severity of either a physical or emotional nature; loving firmness, respect, and warm, genuine affection will always be the most effective communication between parents and their children. But, as usual, when someone crashes the scene with radical, new concepts, vast numbers of advocates carry the new approach to the extreme. Thus, Dr. Spock's book on child- care launched a sharp decline in parental authority, and brought about a steep rise in the number of spoiled, undisciplined children in America. One only has to pick up a newspaper from any city of our nation to realize this problem has grown to desperate and dangerous dimensions.

It suffices to say that situations in both the home and school have become unacceptable if we, as Americans, wish to remain members of a first world nation. It is little wonder that even in difficult economic times, private schools are filled to capacity. Thousands upon thousands of parents are willing to face financial and often personal time-consuming sacrifices in order to offer their children islands of sanity where it is possible to obtain a solid education and discipline that used to be customary in public schools. Private and parochial schools offer no school bus services. If a family happens to live near a public school bus stop, the children area allowed to ride to and from that stop area. This is, of course their right; they pay public school taxes. But, in most cases, parents of private school children are obliged to drive them to and from school, and to any extra- curricular activities in which the children may be involved. The expense of sending a child to a private/parochial school is often draining to a family. Yet, more and more concerned parents are choosing this option.

It is time to take a good, hard look at where we have been, and where we are going. The evidence is overwhelming, and soon we will all pay a huge price. The report of an eighteen member, bi-partisan commission on American education, which found American schools to be sorely in need of improvement, should come as no surprise. When children are no longer safe in many of our nation's schools, when school systems spend nearly as much money on repairing the results of vandalism as they do for textbooks, when we are clothing functional illiterates in caps and gowns, it is time to look at the record of today, and reassess the fundamental tenets of yester-year to intelligently determine what really does help Johnny read!

ADDRESSING THE PROBLEMS

"... for it's the hand
that rocks the cradle
'tis the hand
that rules the world"
(William Ross Wallace)

There are several factors that determine a child's ability to learn to his potential. Most of these exist within the child's life before he reaches the classroom. The social conditions a child inherits are often indicative of his learning capacity. Many urban children are raised in an atmosphere of poverty, crime and drug abuse, which liberals have perpetuated with welfare handouts. Too often, such children arrive at their primary classrooms with predisposed attitudes of mistrust of lofty goals, disrespect for teachers, and a decided lack of motivation to cooperate and learn. In most cases, these very young children carry these preconceived ideas with them straight from their home. It is true, that with high expectations and effective methods of teaching, these at-risk students can extend their reach, but it is difficult for teachers alone to overcome the conditions that hamper such children's progress, because the recognition of the importance of learning in such cases does not originate in the home.

Culture sometimes influences a child's primal perspective of the importance of school and learning. If, for instance, school is a lower priority than contributing to family finances, this learned attitude militates against academic success. In this case, the child may not be behaving in a culturally irresponsible manner by missing school to attend family obligations, but needless to say, he is not learning.

An opposite end of this scenario was illustrated in the high school at which I taught American history, World history, and World geography. Almost ten percent of the school's population was comprised of Oriental students. In nearly every instance, these people were "A" students, although they did not display unusually mature social, communicative, or mental skills. What they did possess was a desire to learn and attain good marks, and to utilize their knowledge through constructive and creative avenues. They were willing to work hard and study diligently to acquire skills necessary to bring their aspirations to fruition. After pondering on what made them so different, I reached the conclusion that they obtained this "effort ethic" from their homes.

About twenty years ago, William Raspberry, a DETROIT NEWS columnist, quoted Janice Hale-Benson as stating that," An African style of learning is 'relational', meaning that such learning features approximation, contextual meaning, and a focus on people, while the European style is analytic, and emphasizes precision and a focus of things"[5]

A good teacher will try different approaches to put a lesson across, and smart teachers not only understand the necessity of building on what a child has already learned, but also to strive to identify the impediments to learning that may be a part of the child's home environment. But the idea that teachers should disperse information according to their students' background and have an obligation to reacquaint students with their cultural styles is pure poppy-cock!

Teachers' duties are to teach and to stimulate a love of learning while recognizing and appreciating the multiple personalities and cultures of their students. However, it is not the duty of the classroom educator to cater to those traits, which are counter productive to effective learning. To state it simply, good education begins at home. The faults found in our education system should not be focused exclusively on teachers.

Children who are raised in city poverty seem to be at a crucial disadvantage. Our socialistic welfare system has so encouraged mental apathy and idleness, that there are now fourth and fifth generations of families who have dropped out of school, married, begotten off-spring, and then have settled back to live in a state of self-hate, self greed, and intellectual lassitude.

I was once employed at a career training school as an admissions representative. I can safely state that at least one third of the prospective students I interviewed had anywhere from one to three children, all born out of wedlock. These young, unwed males and females were raising their babies with welfare money. Their life's philosophy was that everything they wanted should be free, and the more babies they had, the more money they should receive on a regular basis. And these folks were the cream of the crop! These were persons who decided to acquire training in a skill in order to begin to support themselves. Of course, most were not willing to exert themselves to any great degree, and even those who were awarded federal and state grants and loans to pay for their training education often did not start school, or dropped out when it became apparent that they had to actually study.

Children in such families are often abused by ignorant, and sometimes cruel parents. Lack of self- respect is usually generated by lack of gainful usefulness, and if a man has no respect for himself, he generally lacks respect for others as well. This, all too often, results in unfortunate abuse and neglect of pre-school and school age children.

A teacher from the East side of Detroit recently lamented that a regrettably large number of city school children show up for kindergarten not knowing their names. "They only know their nicknames", she said. Another first grade teacher from the same area wanted to hold back twenty four of her thirty students because she had spent most of the year teaching the children how to write their own names. Some, even at the first grade level, didn't even know their names. [6]

We are seeing uneducated, ignorant, immoral babies giving birth to babies, and a sort of "gene-depletion is taking place. Unless the governmental policies of our nation change, and today, it looks as if it will probably get worse than it has been in the past twenty years, due to the vast amount of money being sent out for earmarks for programs so more folks can afford to be idle to an even greater degree, we will continue to be besieged with a fresh layer to our future underclass; spiritually buried persons in prison cells, on welfare rolls and street corners and sometimes in hospital emergency centers riddled with bullet holes from Saturday night specials. We will continue to cringe for kids who are sexually abused, and for toddlers who are tortured by ignorant, soulless, temperamental child-parents. We will continue to build on the junk pile of parasites, who drain our country's economy with welfare handouts, which do not help them gain a better quality of life.

There is the instance of the child who liked school because it was the only place in which he felt safe, but he lived in a moving crack house. This made even showing up for school a difficult procedure because his drug-peddling family kept getting evicted. Once the family moved to a shelter several miles from his school, and he called the school counselor in a panic. The elementary principal was quoted as saying:

"Here's a kid who wanted to come to school. We had to deal with all of this before we could even think about trying to teach him reading and math. [7]

You can be assured that this family, and thousands like them in cities across our country are living as parasites on welfare money from tax dollars that could be used for far more beneficial purposes. This gigantic handout system is definitely not nurturing, nor is it enhancing the lives of most of its recipients. If the liberal public has not shed tears for those wretched individuals who are thrown a bone while they lose their souls, they will indeed shed their money in taxes. Yet, the schools that are facing the many problems caused by our monstrous welfare programs are, for the most part, the ones who espouse politically liberal, even socialistic ideals in their classrooms, and teachers who complain about difficulties in teaching at-risk children consistently cast their electoral votes to continue this madness.

The sexual revolution our American society has experienced over the past few decades has greatly added to the rising numbers and types of problems in the home and classroom. An ever-increasing lack of self-esteem and respect for opposite sexes has taken place and allowed to fester within our culture. Men and women's sexuality is no longer thought of as being sacred and exclusive to the powers of love and marriage. The very definition of love has perfidiously degenerated from ardent desire for life-long commitment, to a superficial sense of immediate self-pleasure. Often today, we hear people say they are in love, but do not want to make the commitment of marriage. I sometimes wonder if our moral values have regressed to the point that many people are really ignorant of love's true emotion, and the role our sexuality plays in genuine love.

Recent history has shown that unmarried, live-in couples, and couples who have married without genuine devotion and respect for each other, have precipitated a sharp rise in spouse and child abuse, and have militated against the type of healthy family atmosphere needed for the emotional, moral, and mental well-being of children. It is impossible for a teacher to expect a child to concentrate on his multiplication table when he is immersed in the fear that his separated father or his mother's live-in boy friend will again crash through the door in the middle of the night to beat up his mother, as had happened the previous night. I faced this very problem with a frightened and confused fourth grade boy. The necessity of comforting him (and later confiding the incident to the school counselor) superseded the importance of multiplication facts. This incident took place in an affluent suburb.

Men and women must return to values of moral responsibility and integrity if society is to function at its best. Immediate pleasure does not always accompany happiness, in spite of what our modern pseudo, self-proclaimed psychologists would have us believe. Parents are indulging themselves as much as they are their children. Since we humans are all born with the inbred need for refining, we must be ever aware of our need for self-discipline, and self-imposed behavioral ethics. Edmund Burke wrote, "Men are qualified for civil liberty in exact proportion to their disposition to put moral chains upon their own appetites." So, parent, if you don't want the government to tell you what you may and may not watch on T.V. or in the movie houses, RESTRAIN YOURSELVES in what you watch and financially support.

The fundamental, basic role model for a child is his parents. Dr. John Bowlby, honorary consulting psychiatrist in London, England in the nineteen nineties, and world renowned expert on relationships between infants and parents, and the impact of these relationships on personality development and psychological disturbances, holds a firm belief that family influences play a major role in mental, emotional, and moral health. His beliefs are bolstered by both clinical experience and documentary research studies. While lecturing to a packed audience of mental health practitioners in our small Michigan town, he explained: "The way in which a person's thoughts, feelings, and behavior develop from infancy onward can be explained by two theories." The first he called 'developmental pathways'. The second theory was what he called 'representative models'.

"Developmental pathways", he said, "refers to the development of personality in a continuous process of interaction by what is genetically given, and what is experienced. It's an interaction between nature and nurture, which begins at conception, and continues until the end of our lives. At any age, a person is a current product of these influences."

Dr. Bowlby described representative models as impressions which we build in our minds; our pictures of our geographical environment and our personal environment. He stated that children build up a representation of our parents very early on. He went on to say, "A child's image of himself is built from his own first-hand experiences, and from input from others, thus parent opinions weigh enormously heavily!" [8]

In addition to his own self-image, a child's image of what a parent should or should not be in relationship to what a parent actually is, signifies an important relevance to his general outlook on life. It stands to reason, for instance, if parents patronize "R" rated movies, a child will perceive that such movies are acceptable. And they will see the behavior in such movies acceptable, also. If parents habitually watch violent or sexually orientated television shows, their children will see no wrong in such behavior. The trick is in finding a T.V. show that is NOT sexually oriented. I will state several times throughout this book, that if sexually violent T.V. shows and movies were not patronized, they would not be offered, and better entertainment would prevail and be at our disposal. Children, especially pre-teen children, are not prone to distinguish between tangible and intangible perceptions in life, so that if they are raised by immoral, unconcerned parents who invite entertainment into their homes that depicts decadent behavior, they will come to believe that what they are seeing and hearing on the television is also acceptable behavior. A four-year-old child is able to discern behavior in something he or she is viewing. As that child grows older, individual behavior becomes more integrated with his or her own life. Today, we have across our great land, pre-teens and teens, who on regular basis, are watching beautiful movie idols have sex. Leading ladies are going to bed with leading men whom they have just met, in the midst of story plots that condone such behavior. Parents witness this silver screen and T.V. depravity, often with their children, and declare at the final scene, "Wow, what a great movie!" What on earth can we expect from their children? We can expect them to behave exactly as their movie idols behave in movies. That's what we can expect! And that, dear readers, is what is happening. It is no surprise that nearly one out of every ten babies born in the United States, are born to unwed mothers. [9]

Since it is vitally important to a child that he believes in the goodness and wisdom of his parents, he will naturally model his behavior after them. Let us agree that it is counter-productive to any child's set of values, for parents to coin the phrase, "Do what I say; not what I do." Children will do what their parents do, and in most instances today, they are doing it at an all too early age. I was teaching a class one day, when my fourth graders came in from recess upset because a dog had been hit by a car, and not yet dead, was writhing in pain. One of the boys laughed about how the poor creature tried to move, and couldn't because its body was broken and bloody. I took him aside, and asked him how he could find humor in such tragic animal pain. He giggled, and said," Oh, my dad and I once hung a live cat, and we watched it die, hanging up there. Dad and I thought THAT was funny!" I informed the lad that such treatment of animals is horribly cruel, and his response was, "No, it isn't. My dad didn't see anything wrong with it." This is an extreme case of parental moral irresponsibility, but there is a wide range of parental behavioral attitudes between that boy's father, and desirable, acceptable behavior.

It is time for American parents to wake up and reappraise their own values of moral standards, if this country is to be a safe and healthy place in which to live. It is time to stop being complacent about the immoral fiber of the entertainment business, and realize that there is a cause and effect relationship in all this. It's time to insist upon excellence in the content and in the context of entertainment offerings, by shunning that which is inconsistent with socially healthy principles. Parents must first demand exemplary deportment of themselves, and then expect it of their children. Americans have begun a backward trend from living civilized and dignified lives, toward becoming uncivilized, immoral, crude examples, and it is showing up in our youths like a perfidious, contagious disease.

The fault of our educational failures does indeed, lie within our schools, but its inception was begun in our homes. If parents do not live morally better lives; if they do not expect morally acceptable behavior from their children, the tasks of teachers are monumental. If parents do not expect excellence of themselves and of their children, then children all across our land will aspire to nothing, unlike the children of yester-year, who DID aspire to the greatness upon which we have, so far thrived, and from whom we have benefited. Sooner or later, the pool of intellect will be depleted. The following quote is from a twenty six year old teaching veteran, told to DETROIT NEWS columnist, George Cantor, nearly twenty years ago.

"When I started teaching, I was the most popular teacher in the school. I was always winning "teacher of the year" votes, conducted by students. Now the word is out that I'm mean. The kids don't want to get me in class, because they know I'll make 'em work! I'll tell you something. Today I assign a fraction of the work I did twenty-six years ago. A fraction! And to these kids, if it takes effort, they're not interested. Even more disturbing to me is the reaction I get

from parents. They're not interested in coming to talk to
you when their kids get a bad grade. Oh, no, not anymore!
Now they go directly to the principal, or in some cases, to
contacts on the school board. The idea that their kid may
need a good, stiff kick in the rear, never seems to occur to
them. If the kid is failing, it must be the teacher's fault.
The A's I give today, would have been C's when I started
teaching, and the C's would have flunked."

Mr. Cantor assured his readers that this woman teaches
in a suburban school district with an excellent reputation.
Mr. Canton says of himself, "When I was going to school, at
a time when children were not worshiped as possessors of
a superior moral and intellectual power, my father would
have taken my head off if I brought home bad grades, and
blamed the teacher for them. That just didn't play. I was
responsible for what I did in school. When I failed geometry
in the tenth grade, because I was goofing off, and was too
dumb to realize I needed glasses to see the blackboard, his
disappointment in me was so acute, that it acted as a spur.
I would never let that happen again."

Mr. Cantor added that another element of failure is
that we have convinced our kids that learning is always
fun. "From the snippets of SESAME STREET to computer
games, we have given kids the message that education is
quick, entertaining, and painless. That's a lie! By the time
you reach high school, learning is work. Sometimes it is
actually inconvenient. There are some things that cannot
be reduced to a game, or mastered in a few snappy lessons.
With permissive, lazy kids, down go the scores. Ours are
near the bottom of industrialized nations, and totally
eclipsed by the kids of our chief economic rivals. But better
not let our kids see that! It may upset them too much to

learn that when they get big, they won't be able to afford playing games on their computers anymore." [10]   He wrote this twenty years ago!

What is lacking today, in homes and in schools, and what Mr. Cantor was alluding to, is accountability! Every person alive must be accountable for his or her actions, and must be liable for their consequences. Accountability is a fundamental, vital ingredient necessary in order for a society to function sanely. Parents are not requiring it of themselves, nor are they forcing their children to be accountable for their actions or words. Schoolteachers and school administrators, instead of insisting that accountability is of paramount importance in acquiring human excellence, are following parental lack of insight. There is such a dangerous trend toward permissiveness in our homes and schools, that honesty, integrity, and decency is thought of, in priorities, somewhere beneath mowing the lawn.

If you do not believe this, ask yourself what abortion is really about. It really does not have anything to do with a woman's right to do with her body, whatever she chooses. Except in the case of rape, by the time she has become pregnant, she has made several choices as to what she wishes to do with her own body. Should she date this person? Should she go home with this person? Should she invite this person into her home? Should she have sex with this person? Should she protect herself from becoming pregnant if she does choose to have sex with this person? A lot of choices! No, abortion has nothing to do with a woman's right to choose what to do with her body. Abortion is really about not being willing to be accountable for the choices she has made in regard to herself and her body. It is about her unwillingness to be held liable for her actions.

So, half of our American population, and now, most of our
government, has deemed it perfectly swell for her to lack
responsibility for her actions, and murder her own child.
That means to scald her own child with acid, or to blow
him or her apart from limb to limb. Or worse, to wait
until this child can suck her thumb, cry if uncomfortable
in the womb, in other words, FEEL both physically and
emotionally, using NO anesthetic, drill a hole in her baby's
head, and suck out his or her brains. All acceptable with
almost half of our society! That is what our country has
come to!

How many folks are incensed over this barbaric conduct?
How many folks disapprove of the many popular T.V. shows
that offer sexual innuendos and sexual permissiveness
throughout their programs?   The theme that permeates
nearly every show is so-called sexual freedom. The fact that
a show's content is crude and vulgar isn't even brought to
the mind of most Americans. In nearly every single show,
the idea that it is okay to have sex before and or outside of
marriage is common fare. It's a "given".

And yet, hundreds of thousands of teenagers watch
these shows every week of the year—week after week!
People are being de-sensitized to immoral behavior. It has
gotten to the point where the majority of folks believe
that there is no sexually immoral behavior. What narrow-
minded person would think otherwise? A study in the
early nineteen nineties of people, who live in and around
Detroit, showed that 98% wrote in to say that they thought
too much sexual voyeurism and crude language was shown
on T.V. Yet, how many of those people chose to turn off
the offending programs and write their sponsors vowing
to never again watch their shows? If folks were asked the

same question today, I venture to say, there would be a very few who would have opined the same thoughts about the offerings on T.V., and today, the shows are even worse.

Let's, for a moment, discuss the language and speech people use today. How many PG 13 movies are simply wonderful, except that, somewhere in the film, someone has to say some foul words? The thinking, of course, is that the same movie would draw a smaller audience if it were not rated PG13 at least. So, in order to dub the movie PG13, some smut needs to be interspersed throughout. Nonsense! Consider the movie THE LION KING, a perfectly wonderful movie that serves as a welcome exception to this notion. I've seen it with my grandchildren several times, and performed some of its songs on stage with the theater group to which I belong. Vast number of parents purchased the video when it went on sale. Although I have to admit that there was one small incident in the film that had a questionable subject; one by the way, the children picked up on immediately. But it was relatively harmless. Hollywood just doesn't know how not to add these things; they think everyone thinks like they do. My point is that movies that did not have smut in them would still be popular. Hollywood just has not caught on to that fact yet.

I believe the problem is compounded by moviemakers who have very little sense of decency, morality, and public responsibility. They simply don't know there is anything wrong in including obscenities in PG or PG13 movies. And parents are not paying much attention to this anymore, because they don't have much of a sense of decency either. It is almost as if Hollywood has formed and molded society to their own depravity. The common response today is, "one can't be a prude—after all, this is the twenty first century."

Very few American families today insist that certain behavior among the family members within their home is simply not tolerated; simply not done. Too many external forces are blamed for a person's behavior; society is at fault, childhood is at fault, race is at fault, racism is at fault, etc. When a person displays an overt lack of respect for another human being, when he cheats or lies, whenever he resorts to immoral acts or speech, it is universally accepted for the perpetrator of such behavior to conjure up reasons as to why he, alone, should not be held responsible and accountable. And sad to say, many public institutions abet this type of twisted logic. Where does accountability teaching begin? It begins right in the home when a child is in infancy, and it should be an on-going lesson given by on-going morally responsible parents throughout entire life- times. If this sounds too demanding, too tough an assignment, I assure you, the consequences of our disciplinary passivity will soon be much tougher to bear.

One day, as I was lecturing to my American history class, I abruptly stopped to wake a student who habitually slept through all of his classes. I had tried everything imaginable to interest this young man in school, from empathetic, good- natured cajolery, to downright anger. I didn't feel this to be a sign of flawed lectures on my part, as most students enjoyed my lectures, and upon occasion, I had the rare pleasure of students from another history class ask to sit in on my lectures. I even had students, who visited from other schools, tell me that they wished I were their teacher. This particular young man was nice looking, with a wonderful personality, and possessed many fine attributes commensurate to personal success in life. We, in fact, enjoyed a friendly teacher-student relationship. He was not only failing my history class, but he was failing nearly every other subject as well. This day I felt a great need to spur him to realize his waste of positive potential. When I spoke sharply to him, decrying his lassitude in regard to learning and grades, he informed me that he planned to be a millionaire, and didn't need history. When I asked him HOW he was going to become a millionaire, he said he didn't know, but he'd think of something. I nearly "lost it" at that point, and loudly responded with, "Exactly how are you going to achieve this financial status without a high school diploma? Or have you decided to sell 'crack' and chance getting yourself killed or put behind bars for several years of your life?"

The next morning the boy's mother, with whom I had been in contact several times about this problem, arrived at the high school principal's office, angry that I had said these things to her boy. Since he was an African American, she called me a racist for intimating that the only way for him to become a millionaire was to sell crack cocaine. She never appreciated that I had tried several times to spur him on to better things in life.

The next day, Dennis Archer, then Chief Justice of Michigan's Supreme Court, and later, the mayor of Detroit, came to speak to the entire high school. He espoused the identical values I had consistently conveyed to all of my students, and to that young man, the previous day. Judge Archer noted that without decent grades in school, there is limited success in the world beyond high school, and that now was the time to put forth every possible effort to learn. I was sitting toward the back of the assembly, and spotted my "class sleeper", who sat several rows ahead. When Judge Archer summed up his oration, the young man turned around, found my eyes, and with a broad grin, gave me the thumbs-up sign. He finally realized what I had tried to do for him. His mother still considered me a racist.

A similar incident happened in the same school. I was always understanding about sports game nights, and knowing that ball players and cheerleaders had very little study time on those nights, I did not give tests or quizzes the following day. I felt that those social activities were important in a child's high school experience. My kids appreciated this consideration. However, I once had the audacity to announce that they would be given a quarter-final test on the day that followed the Grammy Awards telecast. One, eleventh grader stated that it was unfair for me to do so, and she was going to watch the Grammy Awards instead of study for the test. Quarter- final tests carry a lot of clout, grade-wise, so I advised her to reconsider her decision. The class had three days in which to prepare, and of course, we reviewed in class, so it was not as if I had sprung a surprise test on them. I advised her to prepare for the three days, then watch the award presentations for a half hour or so, then turn off the T, V, to concentrate on test review and preparation. (Coincidentally, my own high school daughter also had a test scheduled for that same day, different school, and was similarly "bummed out" that she could not watch the Grammy Awards. I had required of her the same suggestion I had made to my students, whereupon she watched for half an hour, then the television was turned off while she studied and reviewed for her test.)

Test day came and went, and this young lady, who had a B- average going into the test, failed her quarter-final miserably, which lowered her final quarter grade to a D. She was incensed, and informed me that her mother would take of me! The girl, like my "sleeper", was a black person, and I once again, found myself in the principal's office being called a racist; this time for giving the young lady a final quarter grade of "D". I explained that I didn't GIVE her anything; that I only record what my students earn, and her daughter EARNED a "D".

I went on to relate the Grammy conversation I had with her daughter, and the mother's response was, "Well, it's pretty stupid to give a test the day after the Grammy awards. I insist that you change my daughter' grade!" Out of the school she flew, and the next day, the girl's irate father sat in the principal's office, yelling loudly, demanding that I alter the girl's grade. It was one of the worst weeks of my life.

It all boiled down to the fact that the parents of both my sleeper, and this girl, wanted desperately for their children to get good grades, but they felt that their children should not have been asked to work for them. I thought, how sad for both of these black families, who are among so many of all races, striving to find a decent, respected place in today's society, to go about it in such a counter-productive manner for their children. And in both cases, the young people possessed sufficient intellectual equipment necessary for success. To cry "racist" whenever someone pushes a black child to be the best he can be, is to defeat his chances of procuring for himself, a better life. Yet, teachers often face this dilemma, especially in city schools.

An example of such misplaced accusation took place in another of my American history classes, which left me confused, hurt, and angry. Two girls, who were best friends, were among my top students. Their grades were consistent A's; their essays were beautifully written. They displayed excellent performances in all areas of learning, with one exception. They wrote and spoke, as did the families with whom they lived, which is to say, they consistently failed to add the "s" on plural words. They might say, for instance, "It took me three hour to do my homework." These girls were delightful young women. One aspired to be an attorney, the other, a pediatrician. I realized the importance of the ultimate need to speak and write proficiently, so one day, I spoke to each of them after class, and explained my red-penned "s" on all of their plural words. We devised a secret sign for just the three of us. Whenever they spoke in class, and used improper English, I would casually touch my nose or temple. Over the period of just a week or so, it became amusingly clear to them how often they spoke incorrectly. They asked if I would help them overcome this problem, so we agreed to meet after school each day to work on their improvement. As the first week ended, they mentioned another friend who wished to join us, and whom I, of course, welcomed. By month's end, the girls had greatly improved, and had especially embraced the habit of attaching the "s" to plural words. I thought that they did not need my help any longer, but told them I would always be there if they needed any further help in the future.

I was stunned when the principal called me into her office to inform me that a group of parents had decided that I was attempting to obliterate their culture. The poor girls were thoroughly disgusted with this notion, but not more so than I.

As one can deduce from these examples, it is sometimes impossible for a teacher to encourage excellence, or to be influential in a child's reach for his potential, when necessary ingredients are lacking within the home.

One day, as I was substituting for a third grade teacher,

an absurd situation arose. It was clear to me within the first minutes of the morning, that this class was sadly lacking in structure. One child, after having been asked to take his seat, proceeded to throw a temper tantrum, and when he deliberately tipped over his desk, I placed his desk next to mine, and asked him to sit there until he felt better. Within the next hour, this child became so disruptive, it was necessary for me to take him to the principal's office, where, according to the school secretary, he spent a great deal of time.

Later in the day, two little girls got up during a math lesson, and began to play tag in and out of the coat lockers. I asked them to find their seats, and sit down in them. They completely ignored me. So I walked over to them, waited for the first girl to emerge from a locker, caught her by the arm, immediately seized the other girl's arm, and marched them to their seats. I firmly told them,"You must sit at your desk during math class, and you must stay there!"

I was asked to teach again the next day, and when I walked into the office the next morning the principal confronted me with fact that both mothers of these little girls had called to complain that I had yelled at their children, and grabbed their arms. I asked the principal if either of these mothers had inquired as to why my firmness was necessary. Her answer was, "No." She stated that we do not have the legal right to even touch children, no matter how terrible their behavior. The outcome of this discussion led me to discover that teachers in that particular school simply ignored poor behavior. The parents were getting what they asked for, which was classroom permissiveness, the teachers were accommodating the parents, and the children were free to display unacceptable behavior. It is not difficult to deduce that these children were also not learning very much. This particular school was located in a wealthy suburban community.

It puzzles me as to how such parental and teacher lassitude could possibly help those children to be accountable for their actions. Pity the society in which such lack of discipline exists. Pity us! American society has become more and more perilous, primarily because parents and schools are not demanding self-discipline of their children, and are not expecting them to face consequences for improper behavior. Misconduct in the home, and especially in school, creates an atmosphere counter-productive to adequate learning. And what happened to the boy who threw the tantrum, tipped over his desk, and went to extraordinary measures to disrupt the class? Nothing! "Having a substitute teacher always upsets him; he always acts that way," was the principal's explanation. The parents were not even contacted.

As much as I love children of all ages, (I have six of my own, adults now, of whom I am extremely proud), and as much as I love teaching, I find it more and more difficult to abide what is happening in America's classrooms today. I could go on and on with tales similar to those I've just mentioned! Unless parents demand of themselves, then demand of their school systems, to expedite a swift restoration of good, old fashioned values, and unless these values are demonstrated and demanded of children, society as we've known it, and American world authority as we've known it, will crumble before our eyes. When Johnny can't get a decent job; when Johnny can no longer compete in the world market, who shall blame whom for the fact that Johnny cannot succeed because he did not learn well enough in school?

INADEQUACIES IN SCHOOL

n 1989, the National Educational statistics revealed some startling facts about our continuing decline in American scholastic abilities. In reading, three and one half million nine year olds completed third or fourth grade. Over two hundred thousand could not read and understand their textbooks, yet ninety four percent were said to be reading at grade level. Today, the statistics have not changed to any great degree. Each year of the past three decades, about forty percent of eighth graders have had trouble reading and understanding their textbooks. Those statistics have not changed greatly in twenty years. There is a dramatic slip between third and fourth grade, and eighth grade. What seems to be happening to children between the fourth and eighth grades?

During the 1989-90 school year, over three million seventeen year olds were high school juniors and seniors. Almost half of these people had still not mastered eighth grade mathematics upon graduation. In fact, only six percent completed their secondary school proficient in what a generation prior to theirs was considered high school mathematics, i.e., algebra, geometry, and multi-step problem solving. Twenty years later, the statistics have not changed greatly!

In June of 1990, three and one-half million thirteen

year olds finished the seventh or eighth grade in the United
States. One and one -half million of them, about half,
still do not understand basic information from the life of
physical sciences. Fewer than ten percent of our seventeen
year olds leave school with an understanding of biology,
chemistry, and physics. This is to say that ninety percent are
not equipped to pursue engineering and scientific programs
in college. [11] These numbers are still true today.

The writing skills of our high school, and even college
students are greatly disappointing. A conversation with
a friend who deals with the court systems revealed that
young attorneys are sadly lacking in the ability to express
themselves through the written word, and the spelling skills
of these people are atrocious.

Comprehensive skills in both social studies and English
are also lacking among American students. An eighty
seven question examination given to six hundred ninety
six seniors at sixty seven colleges, (not a true representative
sample of total U.S. students, but nonetheless, probably
typical), showed that slightly more than half had heard of
Moby Dick or David Copperfield; only half could identify
the Magna Carta and the Emancipation Proclamation, and
after sixteen years of American education, sixty percent
of these seniors thought the Korean War began during
the Roosevelt administration. One third of these people
confused reconstruction with the Marshal Plan, and one
in four college seniors think that, "From each according to
his abilities, to each according to his needs," (Marx's day-
dream), is from the United States Constitution. [12] Although
our grade school, high school, and college students are in
desperate need of comprehensive skills, most alarming is
that they are profoundly limited in knowledge. It seems

kids today, ARE learning less!

Chester Finn, Jr., one of America's voices concerning education, states that a large part of the problem is that the education profession is pursuing the wrong goals. He says it is obsessed with whether the student's mind is functioning, and is not sufficiently emphasizing the business of actually LEARNING things. He states, "Our educators, in general, are so transfixed by cognitive skill, that they have concluded that as long as you are thinking, it does not really matter whether you KNOW anything; as long as you are reading, it does not matter WHAT you are reading; as long as you are able to analyze, it doe not matter whether you possess knowledge worth analyzing.[13] One simply must know facts in order to form intelligent opinions. Factual information leads to knowledge, and knowledge enables a person to base life decisions of intelligent conclusions.

When teaching American history, I often required my high school juniors to write essays in which they were to discuss their opinions based on the facts they had learned from my lectures, their textbook, and classroom discussions. For instance, if I were to ask them to write their opinions on Hamiltonian philosophy verses Jeffersonian ideals, they first needed to know the beliefs of these two men. They had to know when and how the two political philosophies have crossed each other from today's liberal and conservative thinking, and they needed to know why. (In their day, Hamilton was considered to be a conservative, and Jefferson was thought to be a liberal thinker. Hamilton believed the elite (government) knew what was best for the masses, and Jefferson was a firm advocate of individual rights and self-determination.) Yet today, it is the liberals who defend the idea of government control, and conservatives attempt to protect the rights of the individual, and an individual's right to self-determination. The students needed to know this. They were also required to be familiar with social, economic, and political values at that time in America, and which ideals have changed over the course of the past two hundred years. Thus, my students were expected to possess knowledge of historical facts and the ability to comprehend the significance of what those facts mean in terms of yesteryear and today. So, actually their opinion papers called for intellectual conclusions drawn from facts and experience.

Did my kids like to do this? Heavens no! These exercises necessitated not only real thinking, but also required a great amount of study and review. What was my purpose in assigning such difficult work for them? It was to help them become better, more informed human beings; future voters, who hopefully would cast their election ballots based on intelligent logic from knowing which facets of our government have worked best for our nation, which have failed in American society, and why.

Because I hold a strong belief in the value of effective writing skills, and the needed ability of students to express themselves on paper, I also graded them on sentence structure, vocabulary usage, and grammar. I enjoyed a humorous, informal relationship with my students, and the first part of the year they complained that I was much too "picky". One lad, who received his graded paper, announced, "My poor essay looks like it's bleeding to death!" As I expected, however, as the year progressed, the papers became better and better. Many improved to the extent that they were excellent examples of writing. My biggest thrill at the end of each year was when most of my students confided that they used to hate history, but were now really "turned on" to history. And NONE of them thought I was easy!

America has become soft; soft in moral structure, soft in principles, and extraordinarily soft in regard to accountability.   Parents don't expect it of themselves or their children; educators don't expect it of themselves or their students. One look at the performance and academic advances of other countries points out a dangerous decline in scholastic adeptness here at home.

Gary Phillips, who administered the federal government's National Assessment of Education Process Testing in 1990, said that student scores have remained flat for twenty years. Which is a loss compared with other industrialized nations that have improved student achievement. This is true today. For the last twenty years, U.S. students have finished last of thirteen nations in math scores, and twelfth of thirteen in science.   Albert Shanker, president of the American Federation of Teachers, (ATF) reported that extensive written-answer testing found that ninety five percent of American young adults who go to college would not be accepted at any other college in the world. [14]

California colleges are being faced with a new type of problem. Whereas that ultra-liberal state once advocated strong measures of affirmative action regarding race a few decades ago, demanding an equal proportion of blacks to whites in their universities, they are now involved in the dilemma of practicing fair acceptance policies in regard to white students vs. Asian students. It seems that, although nine percent of California's high school students are Asian- American, about twenty six percent of Berkley's undergraduates are Asian- Americans. You see, Asian American students strive hard to achieve academic excellence. This has the white population of Berkley so upset that they have revised the formula by which applicants are evaluated. Because Asian- Americans possess a great respect for education and learning, and are willing to work hard toward academic achievement, Asian- Americans lead all other ethnic groups in the United States, including "Wasps" in educational attainment. [15]

America is falling farther and farther behind in technological advances. "Even as telecommunications are revolutionizing the political and economic world, in what the FINANCIAL TIMES OF LONDON calls 'a picture of relentless change', says Warren T. Brooks of THE DETROIT NEWS, "The United States, once dominant position in this market, has been fading fast. Together, Europe, Canada, and Japan now outstrip the U.S. total with seven of the top telecommunications equipment manufacturers in the world." He goes on to say, "It would be ironic in the extreme if the information revolution, spawned by U.S. technology and now democratizing the world, were to leave the United States a second-rate economic power." [16]

In order for our nation to remain politically, militarily, and economically strong, we must expect more of our future technicians, namely, our children. Less than three percent of our college students are majoring in math or science, and less than two percent of high school graduates go on to college to become engineering graduates. [17] It stands to reason there is no hope of keeping pace in the world market with such sorry statistics. Such serious lagging behind other nations of the world should be a primary concern to all Americans who care about the future of next generations. The fact of the matter is, Johnny can't read. Johnny can't write. Johnny doesn't know where Tokyo, or Vienna, or Ankara is. He cannot compete with a German child or an

Asian child, because he has not learned the fundamentals in our American schools, and he has not been encouraged at home, or at school, to aspire to do so.

Because of Johnny's inadequacy, the United States is being dragged down, and if things do not improve, our country will, indeed, become a second world nation. The less Johnny learns, the less he earns, which means American taxpayers must make up for his inability to meet his financial responsibilities. Also, when Johnny is living on welfare, or Aid to Dependent Children, or some other social handout, he develops a great lack of self-esteem, which, as recent indications reveal, often leads to a life of crime. Our jails and prisons are filled with such "Johnnies", and these over crowded institutions are costing the American taxpayer millions of dollars, which in turn, is crippling our nation's economy more with each passing year.

According to an article in the READERS DIGEST, Princeton University professor, John Dilulio Jr., states," I asked a group of long and life-term prisoners what was triggering the explosion of violence among the new, young criminals. I didn't hear the conventional explanations, such as poverty or joblessness. Instead, these hardened men cited the absence of people---family, adults, teachers, preachers, coaches---who would care enough about young males to discipline them. In the vacuum, drug dealers, and 'gangsta-rappers' serve as role models..." This article points out, that from 1985 through 1993, while the murder rate by adults over twenty five and older dropped by about twenty percent, it increased by sixty five percent among eighteen to twenty four year olds, and soared to a terrifying one hundred and sixty five percent among fourteen to seventeen year olds. It stated that in 1995, there were 7.5

million males ages fourteen through seventeen; there are over five hundred million young men of those ages today in our society. Furthermore, in the same article I found this chilling statistic, excerpted from a study published in the journal, HEALTH AFFAIRS: each murder costs society $2.4 million, each rape, sixty thousand dollars, and each assault, twenty two thousand dollars. [18] Today, those numbers have almost doubled.

Many large American corporations are finding that the problem of academic dysfunction of American young people is costing them, too. A great number of companies spend hundreds of thousands of dollars each year in training, which they say would not be necessary if their young employees were better educated. Even in factories, a person needs to be adept at such skills as reading instructions, and filling out order forms in an articulate fashion.

In 1995, the Chrysler Corporation spent over one hundred twenty million dollars training its work force, and at least ten percent went toward teaching their employees the "three R's" they should have learned in school. The Chrysler Corporation was not alone in this endeavor. Today, all of the American industries together, spend more money each year teaching remedial math to U.S. workers than all the grade schools, high schools and colleges spend on math education.

Yet money for education is not the real solution to the problem. The United States spends more of our gross national income on education than all of our overseas competitors, including Japan and Germany, though functional illiteracy in Japan runs about five percent, while here in America, it is almost twenty to thirty percent. In answer to those folks who claim that poverty is the primary cause of illiteracy, I say look to the recently emancipated Soviet Union, where poverty is a massive problem. Yet, up to 2005, Russia's illiteracy rate has been less than five percent. [19]

Have no doubt! There is a very real problem with the lack of scholastic proficiency in this country. The reasons are varied and complex; more varied than complex, if common sense would only prevail in our land. Now is the time to look at the mistakes that have been made, and put forth an all-out effort to correct them.

Part II

HOPE FOR THE FUTURE
We Can Learn From Mistakes

THE HOME ENVIRONMENT

"Return to the Goodness of the Hearth"

Hope springs eternal in the hearts of the optimistic. But only when hope is applied with positive, reformed action, does improvement take place. From all the tried and failed experiments of child rearing, we certainly should have learned by now that change does not always mean progress, and "new" does not always promote improvement. An in-depth scrutiny of past experiences and experiments, coupled with a critical examination of modern concepts and metaphysics is vital in acquiring a positive, healthy balance.

It has been pointed out time and again, that a child's personality development is influenced first and foremost, by his family. A child's conception of who and what he is, how valuable he is as an individual, and his entire system of mental and emotional health is derived from parental attitudes and response. Parental love is, or should be, naturally inherited in the birth of the human soul. Parenting SKILLS have to be learned. In a country that requires lessons and license to drive a car, hunt game, and even fish, there is no skills requisite for parents who give birth to a human being. In years past, these skills were given to us by prior generations who were received appreciatively by their adult children. In the days when age- old wisdom was respected and cherished, parental knowledge of HOW to love a child was accepted and applied by new generations of mothers and fathers.

Since the nineteen sixties, this process of enlightenment has been degraded. Throughout man's history, there has always been a degree of rebellion of parental authority and convention by new generations; it is a natural process by which young adults attain personal growth and independence. But the radical anti-establishment of the sixties and seventies brought a breaking away from nearly all conventional customs and traditional practices. This was the first generation to eschew almost everything their parents had to offer.

When I taught high school American history in the late 1980's, I thought it would be fun to have a sort of "historical sing-along", beginning with the Revolutionary War, through the Civil War, both World Wars, etc., because so many of our songs have reflected the times in which they were popular. I became sadly aware that these young people were not even vaguely familiar with songs sung by several past generations. When they declared that they were not THEIR songs, I explained to them that many songs I know and enjoy are not songs of my youth, but songs passed down to me by parents and grandparents, and while, in my youth I didn't fully realize it, these songs were accepted as pleasurable additions to my life experiences. It seems these songs died with the parents of adolescents of the sixties. It is sad to realize that today's generation of children are the first ones in American history to know ONLY their current forms of music. What wonderful, rich lore they are missing; not to mention the great musical scores they have eschewed.

Learned and experienced wisdom of many other areas of living have been shunned as well, including learned parental knowledge that could have, and should have, been passed to new mothers and fathers. Young people of today become defensive if parents so much as make a suggestion, so the parents often shy away from offering any wisdom whatsoever. Thus, knowledge is virtually kept from new parents for the simple reason that it is not worth the risk to grandparents to be treated with angry distain. Yet, I remember feeling grateful for any helpfulness my mother and mother-in-law gave to me.

But that was before the mid sixties! Today, we often hear panicked outbursts from young adults crying, "Oh, God, I sound just like my mother!" A condition just too horrible to contemplate! It is such a common lament that it is difficult to acknowledge that before the sixties, people aspired to be as wise, or as good as their parents. An oft-times quoted letter to Ann Landers states quite eloquently, the general attitudes of young people toward their elders, who are able to share so much wisdom and experience;

"We are probably the only members of society in history for which the younger generation has so little respect, and has demonstrated such a shameful lack of regard. Senior citizens are constantly being criticized, belittled and sniped at for every conceivable deficiency of the modern world, real or imaginary. Upon reflection, I would like to point out that it wasn't the senior citizens who took the melody out of music, or the beauty out of art, or the pride out of appearance, or the romance out of love, the commitment out of marriage, the responsibility out of parenthood, togetherness out of family, learning out of education, loyalty out of Americanism, service out of patriotism, the hearth out of the home, civility out of behavior, refinement out of language, dedication out of employment, prudence out of spending, or ambition out of achievement. And we certainly are not the ones who eliminated patience and tolerance from relationships." [20]

While numerous books on child -care have been written and read, thousands of parents in our country do not read them. It would be wonderful if all high school students were required to take and PASS child care classes before being allowed to graduate. Some hospitals do teach women how to change a diaper, bathe and clothe, hold and feed their new child, but due to unreasonable medical charges and greedy insurance companies, this has to take place within the first twenty-four hours after giving birth. Some insurance companies require hospitals to kick the new mother out of the hospital twelve hours after she gives birth to her baby, which means she is probably too groggy and sore to pay much attention to such instructions. So hospital help with baby care is not sufficient either, and books, though very helpful, do not answer spontaneous questions about specific problems at hand. If new parents are not fully aware of normal baby and child development, they often become frustrated in their efforts to care for their baby properly. This often leads to unjust and unrealistic expectations of the baby; sometimes in out-right abuse to the poor child. It is vitally important that new parents are knowledgeable about the mental and psychological needs and growth of a child; seemingly insignificant facts, like why a baby cries, normal bodily functions at specific ages, degrees of warmth necessary to his well-being, when he can visually focus, when he first smiles, why he smiles, when he first coos, (a sign of trying to talk) and what promotes a child's desire and ability to communicate and respond.

My nephew and his wife, when she was pregnant, constantly talked and sang to their unborn baby. After their baby girl was born, they carried on-going conversations with their tiny child; adult conversations--- no baby talk for them---while they bathed, fed, and rocked her. Both parents frequently laughed and chatted with their baby, displaying genuine affection for her as a highly worthwhile human being. By the age of two, she was a calm, well-adjusted, happy child who spoke in articulate, multi-word sentences. These beautiful parents utilized wisdom taught by their parents, as well as new knowledge learned from modern sources of discovery.   I am happy to say that my own children have shown the same insightful, nurturing parental behavior toward their off-spring, and my grandchildren have consequently displayed the same results, such as talking at a very early age, using clearly understood, complex sentence structure. Each one of my grandchildren has a healthy sense of self-worth, and a personality that depicts poise when in the presence of others of all ages.

All parents can practice such care giving to their offspring if educated to do so. Of course, exemplar examples of THEIR parents are the best lessons learned, but I firmly believe that, if that is not available, hospitals and doctors who care for pregnant women, should promote in-depth, mandatory programs for new parents before they are allowed to take their new, helpless individuals into their sole care. These simple programs would be extremely helpful in teaching new mothers and fathers what to expect of and from their child throughout his different stages of life, and what should be expected of them as parents as responders to the various phases of a child's physical and psychological growth.

I had the experience of spending a weekend with, among others, a young couple and their eight- year old son. It was a gala trip to an aquatic amusement park, and we were all in a carefree mood. Upon arrival, we were out of the cars, suitcases in hand, and were in the process of stepping into the elevator, which would take us to our rooms. The young eight-year-old boy immediately stepped to the elevator buttons to become (Otis) himself, and the door began to close just as his father finished walking into the elevator. One of two scenarios could have taken place. Unfortunately, the wrong one did. The boy was trying to hold the doors open, and eventually his father automatically re-opened them. The boy, who did not know about the "hold" button, said, "Oh, sorry, Dad." His father responded with a very angry, "Oh, that's only my right leg you damn near smashed! Get the hell away from there, and let someone who knows what they're doing work the elevator doors". Needless to say, a pall descended upon all of us. What had just been a cheerful, carefree group of five adults and three children, became a tense, uncomfortable group.

Here is what could have, and should have taken place. When the doors began to shut on the father, he should have realized that his son did not purposely close them. It was really no big deal, anyway. That sort of thing happens all the time to folks, and I would chance to bet that if someone other than his wife or son were manning those elevator buttons, that man would have responded much differently.

Once in the elevator, he could have shown the lad the "door open" or "door hold" button, and cheerfully explained how to keep the doors open until everyone was safely in the elevator. What would this have accomplished? For one thing, we could have had our own private "elevator guy" to hold the doors for us. The child would have learned a new fact about elevator doors. He would have felt good about himself, and learned and shared a new skill taught to him by a loving father who valued and respected him as a worthwhile person. Plus, he would have enjoyed playing "elevator guy", thereby enriching his weekend trip, and creating lovely memories.

What did the father's immature and temperamental behavior cause? First of all, it set a tense tone for the entire weekend for all of us. The other two children, whose parents were loving and kind, did not know what to make of this angry atmosphere. The poor little boy, who was obviously used to such treatment, did not respond in any fashion. He had learned to "not feel." He was, however, left with feelings of shame, unworthiness, inadequacy, and a total lack of self-esteem. No wonder he constantly came to us for affection.

The next day, we all traipsed down to breakfast, all of us chatting merrily about the fun day we were about to begin. The eight-year-old lad turned around to say something to me at the same time I happened to be speaking to someone else. His father hit him across his head and told him, "Shut your God-damned mouth! You don't talk when someone is talking!" I then put my arm around the boy, and we all pretended not to have noticed, for the child's sake, but I think, to this day, that we all should have noticed enough to have said something to that parent. The temperamental, angry behavior continued throughout the entire weekend. Developmentally, that poor child would have been better off staying home to play with his batman figures, which he loved to do.

That one weekend taught him, in his mind, that he was not nearly as important as other children, for the other children in our small group were treated with love and respect. He learned that he could do very little that was right or good, and about the only thing he knew how to do was to make his father angry. All of this knowledge has been stored within his being, amassed with other events in his life, and other responses from his parents. When he becomes an adult, he'll know how to hit, and criticize youngsters, and he'll know how to shame those smaller than himself. He'll know how to be cruel and angry, and he will probably teach HIS children those same ugly traits. It is my guess that HIS father had a similar dad.

The entire weekend could have been such an enriching experience for that young boy. If there had been true affection shown to him, he would have learned that he was a loveable person, and he would have learned to love. As it was, he only learned how to be angry. I saw no occasion where his father put his arms around his son, kissed him, or laughed with him to show him how much he loved spending time with him. If these wonderful displays of affection and respect had taken place, that child probably would never have to do foolish or dangerous things in his teen years to prove himself an important person.

Respect, love, and affection show a child how to be a leader of good activities, and show him that he has abilities to succeed in life, and to occupy a worthwhile place in this world. Possessing these feelings will enable him to seek a high level of happiness with confidence.

Grandparents, help your adult children in the awesome responsibility of parenthood, as your parents did (or should have done) for you. Share your knowledge and expertise, not in a forceful, obtrusive manner, but with love and encouraging support. If possible, talk to your grandchildren about years gone by; about what philosophies seemed to work for people and society, and what types of thinking didn't; what has generally caused happiness and joy, and what situations seemed to create unhappiness and discord. Tell them stories of the past that only grandparents can tell, and try to include in these tales subtle, moral lessons. Your years of life and experience hold a wealth of knowledge and wisdom. Share it with those you love!

Young parents, listen to what your parents share with you. It is not necessary to sacrifice your authority as parents of your own children, to lend an ear to tried and true advice. Open yourselves up to ideas that have worked for generations. Remember those things that helped you gain wholesome confidence and encouraged you to be a better person. And yes, if prudent, discard the passé concepts, which are no longer applicable or judicious today. Age-old wisdom shared is something of precious value. Embrace it, evaluate it, look beyond the immediate to see where it is headed, and draw upon the building blocks of experience.

It is so important that we return to a life that embraces moral values. It is absolutely true that social attitudes develop gradually. One step leads to another; one socially approved value, broken down, ultimately leads to a further breakdown. We did not jump from Victorian, pristine customs to openly accepted codes of behavior, such as live-in boyfriends and girl friends in a day, a week, a year. Common sense and future consequences must be considered when predicting eventual, unfavorable outcomes from current behavioral patterns. It is important to remember that there is a universal cause and effect for everything. I dare to say that before premarital sex was considered socially acceptable; when marital sex was considered sacred and private and beautiful, there were far less rapes, child related sexual abuses, and spousal abuse. In years past, the human body and the human spirit were revered. People possessed a sense of self-respect, and respect for others. If one does not respect self, it is difficult to feel a deep regard for others. The moral code of our culture must reform if we do not wish for our nation to become even more decadent than it is today.

A major improvement could take place for all of us if everyone rarely, if never, supported "R" rated, or even some PG13 movies or T.V. series and shows that display unacceptable social decorum. When adults, and especially children, watch and listen to movie idols and their favorite T.V. personalities use obscene language, or perform violent or sexually promiscuous acts, they naturally identify with these stars. It tells them that, even though they are just acting, they must condone the behavior.

In the 1990's, a WASHINGTON POST article quoted a nationwide survey of ten-to 16-year olds, one third of whom said they often wanted to try things they had seen on T.V., while two thirds said their contemporaries were influenced by what they see on the tube (21) Remember, children of all ages, think primarily with a tangible thought process. They are rarely capable of using intangible logic. Be assured, they will try what you watch and what you allow them to watch. And, as one step leads to another, as has been proven over the years, they will probably go a step or two farther. So if your daughter becomes pregnant, or is raped, and you have habitually watched questionable T.V. programs, or supported violent or sexually graphic movies,

YOU have played a major role in promoting the sort of society in which these horrible things happen. The time has come for parents to become accountable. It is time to quit making excuses as to why "something went wrong" with your child.

I mention self-esteem as a tool with which to remain morally correct. Parents, teach your children to like and respect themselves by giving them a sense of self-worth. Start when they are very young. A person acquires a feeling of self-worth by being shown and told he is valuable. There are many, many circumstances, which can be found in everyday events of which we can take advantage.

A picture appears in my mind with regard to this subject; a memory of one of my small boys, when he was not yet three years old. I had planted alliums in the garden the year before; six bulbs at eight dollars apiece. I cheerfully looked forward to their large, purple blossoms, and when they finally did bloom, I loved to look out of my kitchen window at them. I was able to enjoy their beauty for only two days, however, because on the third morning, I peered out to see my wee lad, with a delighted smile on his face, reach up to pluck them one by one. I started to fly out the door to tell him not to ever pick those garden flowers, but in that fleeting moment, I realized that I had not yet explained to him, which flowers were allowed to be picked, and which were not. The look on his face told me his intent, so I waited in the kitchen as he pushed open the door with his arms full of allium blossoms. He wore an unforgettable grin, as he held them out to me, and said, "I wuv you, Mommy. These are for you."

What a perfect chance for me to encourage his sense of worth. I told him how I loved his beautiful present to me, and what a nice and thoughtful boy he was to present me with such a wonderful gift, and that my morning was happier because of him. Together we put them in a floater vase with water, and placed them on the dining room table. Six huge allium balls were our centerpiece for as long as they lasted. The seeds did not have time to drop to the ground to germinate, so there were none the next year, but I was left with something far more precious; a little boy, who on that beautiful summer morning, had taken a big step to becoming a decent, fine, Air Force Academy graduate, and who is, today, filled with a sense of self-respect and integrity. Although we now laugh about the episode, that summer morning offered a chance for encouragement to be giving and thoughtful, and that was a good thing to be. Needless to say, the next day found us casually strolling through the garden admiring the flowers, and pointing out the ones that should not be picked.

Accentuating the good in a child is far more beneficial than pointing out the bad. This does not mean that firm discipline is not sometimes in order. It does mean that when firmness is necessary, children respond by knowing in their hearts they are valuable human beings, and you will not allow them to become bad; they are much too precious for that!

Empowering our children with self-esteem and self-respect must take place in conjunction with the teaching of respectful behavior. If they are forced to behave well, they, in turn, will enjoy a feeling of self-respect, which will cause them to be less likely to feel a need to prove they are the biggest, the best, the toughest, and the roughest. All of this is a continuous responsibility of parents to their children from infancy, through their teen years, and into their adulthood. And remember, they are looking at you, their parents, for examples.

In a society such as ours, in which there is an incredibly high cost of living, it is difficult for me to say to you mothers, "Stay home with your pre-school children." Nonetheless, this is what I recommend. Your young ones do not need name brand clothes as much as they need a mother's daily presence. Too many babies are being farmed out, and too many children are being raised by virtual strangers. Your matching living room sectionals will wear out eventually; your children, God willing, you will always have. There is no such thing as "quality" time to a child, if the proper "quantity" time is not there. There is, to a child, constant time, with the stable, safe, constant atmosphere of a loving home life. Consider that if most mothers stayed home to raise their own children, the cost of living would decrease, because soon no one would be able to pay the prices they pay today, and product prices would alter accordingly. Also, husbands would earn a better living than they do now, with fewer hours spent in the work place, because there would be a decided decline in the work force, and fewer choices employers would have in the hiring pool.

There have been myriad studies that have shown that working people today spend more stressful hours at work for less money than they did four or five decades ago. Why? Forty or fifty years ago, women worked in the home and raised their own children. The work force was half of what it is today. Corporations were not deluged with employees of both sexes. They had to treat their employees well because there was not such a huge pool from which to choose replacements as there is today. Also, we are paying retail prices geared toward two income families. Make no mistake about it, products from automobiles to milk, would cost consumers much less if there were only one wage earner per family. The price of consumer goods would have to be geared toward the buying power of the consumer.

It is also unfortunate that mothers are working more hours for less pay. The dollars saved are even fewer when one considers the cost of child- care, and career dress attire. Trite as it may seem, a mother also lacks time to take advantage of special sales. If she is employed at the work place, she has little time to frequent stores, thus she is unable to save money on household expenses. These factors offer evidence that the small financial gains that are attained through a mother's career are often not worth the numerous problems caused.

Trend watchers have noted that mothers, the primary nurturers of the young, are nurturing their careers as much, if not more, than they are nurturing their children. Instead of giving their children cultural experiences, they are teaching them how to open bank accounts. The result is that young people do have bank accounts, but are morally and emotionally bankrupt. Character, not capital is what is necessary for behavioral achievement. What children need as requisites for educational success, are not found in designer jeans. They are found in character traits.

An article by Patricia Summerside, former research analyst for the Dakota State Legislature, has stated that her state of South Dakota ranks dead last in average teacher salaries, but scores fifth in the ACT tests among twenty-eight states that take the test. She points out that South Dakota has three things going for it: 1) Families stay together,2 Schools are small, and are centers of community life, and 3) Old fashioned values, such as hard work, responsibility and self discipline still dominate. [22] Home must be a place in which renewed emphasis on basic American values are instilled. Parents must dedicate themselves to LIVING and TEACHING of values such as honesty, a work ethic, self discipline, self control, personal responsibility, sense of duty, and charity, respect for others and the law, love of country and suitable use of its freedom within the context of moral restraint.

Allow me to offer random bits and tips for a rewarding and fulfilling parenthood experience. Talk, sing, cuddle, coo, and in every way, communicate with your newborn. Your baby may look blank and unaware, but within that seemingly unresponsive exterior lies a spirit that is hungrily taking in and processing every sound, feel, mood, touch, smell and taste. Each hour of each day he reacts to his environment; how his environment makes him feel, and stores within his being, his perception of how his small world of people react to him. This "storage" process begins even before birth, and continues until he dies.

Everything a person encounters in life plays a role in what makes that person who and what he is, but what he experiences from birth through five years of age affects him most of all. A child learns to love by being shown love. A child learns compassion by seeing others show compassion. A child learns respect by being given respect by those closest to him. It is important to note, that your respect for your child does not always come with a "yes".

Play with your child, whatever his age. Laugh with him, clown with him, and show him you think that he is a grand person to be with. Dance with him, color with him, play ball with him. Let him know you get a kick out of him. If he makes a mistake of any kind; states a grammatical error or some typical misconception, (common among children, and often humorous) correct his mistake in a loving, casual way so as to downplay the error, and emphasize what a great kid he is. I am, of course, speaking of both girls and boys. It makes a young person feel comfortable if he is told of something similar that you thought when you were about his age. Chuckle at yourself over your own childhood misconception. But never, never make fun of, or in any way humiliate your child. For years, perhaps even for a whole lifetime, he will remember and hate how you made him feel, though you'll never know about his long-harbored feelings, because he will never tell you.

Share the feelings of your spirit with your children. Discuss, at their level, attitudes and philosophies of life. If you are Christian, go to church as a family, and share the life and teachings of Christ. If you are Jewish, go to Temple, and share with your children, your wonderful, ancient traditions and rich heritage. Whatever your religious or spiritual beliefs may be, incorporate them into your family life. If you have no religious beliefs, then share the beauty of a morning sunrise, the majesty of a mighty oak, the splendor of powerful ocean waves. All of these experiences enhance sensitivity within one's soul, and create spiritual awareness, which leads to the development of character. Growth of character leads to the formation of scrupled values, which in turn, results in the kind of citizenship we all admire and honor. These things, you have within your power, to give to your children. If these attitudes were learned in homes throughout our nation, we would indeed, see an improved breed of children entering school classrooms, armed with skills and propensities to aspire to greatness.

SCHOOL ENVIRONMENT

Turn Back To Progress

Let's allow out thoughts to travel back to when Johnny emerged from his grade school, fully prepared for the mental demands of high school; back to when going to school was a given luxury; when learning was difficult, and no one said it was not supposed to be. Think back to when children were taught to respect authority and respect themselves. Think back to the days when it was the duty of students to maintain a clean and orderly classroom. Remember the days when the only thing a teacher had to be concerned about was teaching; when serious discipline problems didn't exist, because they were simply not allowed, so that little stood in the way of learning.

It sounds euphoric when we compare the past with today's scenario, yet most of our current educational problems do not have to continue. Too many modern teachers meet students on the students' terms. The "disadvantaged" and disruptive now rule our schools. Too many parents are setting the terms by which a teacher may exercise discipline, and of course, the kids are very aware of this. Children abuse their school buildings, their classrooms, and their books, loaned freely to them. Where is the pride in their school and in the books, which were so hard to come by years ago? Where is the accountability for poor behavior? It certainly is not with the students! Parents are making sure of that! When schools are filled with graffiti and dirty halls, and classrooms are furnished with carved up desks, it is the taxpayers who put everything back into working order. Parents and teachers take note - You are taxpayers!

Perhaps we could rekindle a spirit of pride in our school children. We could begin by expecting each class to be responsible for its room. Grade school children could be held accountable for their respective rooms, and high school kids, responsible for their homerooms. If or when a room becomes unkempt or defaced, that group of students should devote their own (supervised) time to restore it to its original presentable condition. It is probably safe to say they will not like doing this at first, but I venture to say, that if parents would uphold and encourage this form of accountability, and school personnel stand firm in the face of parental coddling, the children will gradually develop a sense of personal pride in their school surroundings. Most often in life, if a person puts forth his own effort into a project, he becomes personally involved with the results. The children will be far less likely to destroy the fruits of their own labor, and accountability will be placed in the proper hands.

That done, let's examine the lack of discipline in the classroom. Academic and behavioral discipline cannot be attained without the tutored value of self-discipline. Participatory citizenship can be enhanced in this area in the same manner as the development of personal and school pride. Peer pressure is a powerful force in every age group, and can be utilized effectively if approached with positive enforcement procedures. It should be the responsibility of the teacher to first earn the respect of her students, by displaying a sense of fairness and respect toward them. At the same time, she must introduce a formula, by which each student is forced to be accountable for his own behavior. Assertive discipline works well in attaining behavior modification, if it is employed with absolute consistency, and if the classroom and school-wide rules are clearly spelled out at the very beginning of the school year. For example, if a child disrupts the class by talking to his neighbor when it is a "quiet" time, or leaves his seat for no good reason, etc., he is given a warning with the understanding that his next warning will result in some sort of punishment such as extra work while everyone else has "free" time in class, or losing his recess. He would also understand that, yet another infraction of the rules would result in harsher punitive measures, and perhaps parents would be notified if the child would persist in misbehaving. If the situation becomes serious enough for parental contact, I propose that it is firmly suggested to the parents that they come to the school to talk to the principal and the teacher about their child's poor behavior.

The procedure of assertive discipline sounds very simple, and it is if the teacher stays alert to EVERY infraction, and is consistent with the punishments. It is amazing how students adapt to specific rules if forced to obey them, and how soon they alter their behavior accordingly. The key priority here is to clarify each school and classroom rule, and allow the students to fully understand the precise consequences of infractions against each of these rules, and I repeat, to maintain steadfast consistency in carrying out the disciplinary consequences.

I truly do not know why more teachers fail to use this form of classroom management. Several reasons come to mind, none of which are sound rationales. Many educators steer away from a set form of classroom control because they are unwilling to face protective and rationalizing parents. Often teachers do not have the support of weak principals who are easily swayed by parental domination. Sometimes, teachers experience a real fear of being unpopular with their students. Nearly all persons who go into the teaching profession, do so because they have a genuine fondness for children, and enjoy relating to them. They approach their students with the best of intentions, believing they are displaying compassion, when they are actually militating against their students' abilities to soar to greatness. Coddling children behavior-wise and grade-wise merely enables them to think in terms of mediocrity.

One day when I was substituting for a third grade teacher, I was so appalled at the uproarious behavior of most of the children, that during my lunch hour, I spoke to the school principal about them. It was important to me that I appraise the situation as to whether I was lacking in the ability to maintain order, or whether this rowdy behavior was routinely allowed by their regular teacher. The principal's answer to me was," Well, you know, children, like we women, have been liberated." I inquired, "Liberated for what?"

In no way were those third graders given the opportunity to learn near their mental capacity in that chaotic atmosphere. Once again, the theory that the primary ingredient for student academic success was "fun in the classroom" took precedence over the common sense fact that to promote a high standard of scholastic performance, a teacher must enforce the idea that significant learning and personal growth come from hard work, persistence, and self-discipline. She must not enable them to do less.

The function of enabling has been addressed in many self-help associations; the most familiar of which is Al-Anon, the wonderful support group for family members of alcoholics. Enabling also occurs in the classroom. Whenever a teacher fails to set socially acceptable standards for her students, and whenever a teacher fails to hold her students accountable for anti social behavior, that teacher is guilty of enabling her students to continue to perform in unacceptable ways. Enabling is a dangerous deterrent to a child's growth and self-esteem. It can take place in regard to a child's academic behavior as well as his social actions.

In the high school where I taught social studies, the principal expressed her hope that teachers think twice before failing any student. She was a charming and compassionate woman who believed that everyone should feel good about himself, and a student's self-esteem would be devastated if he were to fail a course. She reasoned that the way to prevent this was to always pass students in each of their subjects. I mentioned that it would not take long for the entire school population to realize they would never fail a course regardless of their achievement, or lack thereof, and many would take advantage of this permissiveness, and abate their efforts. It was already evident that the students performed according to which teachers expected most from them, and which teachers were easy.

I had a student who was not receiving passing grades in many of his classes. The principal suggested to me that I give him a special test, or perhaps just part of the test that I gave to the rest of the class. She reasoned that this would keep the boy from becoming frustrated. I flatly refused to comply with such nonsense. How could this young man develop a healthy sense of self-esteem if he were expected to do less than his classmates? What the principal didn't know until I enlightened her, was that I had spent extra time with the student so he could pass the regular test. He finally admitted to me that he hated to study, and sort of gave up when he consistently earned failing grades. Well, I was not about to enable him to use such lack of effort in my class! I helped him to learn good study habits by mapping out a time schedule for his after-school activities, and offered him suggestions for a quiet, distraction-free environment. I also alerted him to the fact that I planned to call on him often in class, so he had better come to class prepared. Then I carried out my promise. When he earned a C- on his semester exam, we were both elated. It was probably the best that boy was capable of accomplishing, and a C- is far from failing. He felt a personal pride and self-esteem he never would have experienced, had he taken an "easy" test designed just for him. So you see, children cannot easily shirk social and academic responsibilities if parents and teachers do not enable them to do so.

Jessie Jackson once wrote of a teacher he once had. "We complained constantly in Mrs. Sheldon's class because she had high expectations, and refused to compromise with us. ' You can complain all you want outside,' she would say, 'but inside this classroom you will apply yourselves, and I will NEVER teach down to you One day, one of you little rascals may run for governor or president, and you WILL be prepared!' She said that to us twelve years before the Voting Rights Act guaranteed African Americans the right to vote. Mrs. Sheldon knew, that just because you were born in the slum, does not mean that the slum was born in you." [23]

We all like to be heroes to those with whom we spend a great deal of time. What parents and teachers should realize is that adults must think and behave as adults, not as hungry egos searching for approval. It is the responsibility of all adults to be good role models, and educators especially, can foster student responsibility and self-esteem by modeling positive classroom expectations.

It is time to stop coddling children, and it is time to stop passing and graduating illiterates who are costing America millions of dollars each year. Let us not debase the worth of the high school diploma to the extent that anyone who cannot read or write can attain one. We must realize that our school children aren't working very hard because they are not being encouraged--- not being expected to do so. Parents and educators from diversified communities across the nation must recognize the unique worth of each individual, and must work to develop in each a sense of honesty, integrity, responsibility, respect for others and for self, and a willingness to be accountable for behavior. When these things are accomplished, when there is order and tranquility and therefore attentiveness in the classroom, learning will take place.

How each subject is taught is of equal importance as is the atmosphere in which it is presented. The following pages offer suggestions for the promotion of scholastic excellence in the various academic disciplines.

READING

There have been many areas in which modern educators have experimented with basic, fundamental skills, and I believe reading is a subject of major concern. Remember the open classroom of the sixties and early seventies? The result of this fiasco showed children's reading abilities to be rapidly slipping in proficiency, so of course, new measures needed to be taken. It apparently did not occur to educators to return to the methods used when reading ability was good, so they decided to move forward to new horizons in teaching reading skills.

Phonics, the basis from which all of us read, was completely discarded, and has not yet regained the popularity it deserves. When anyone reads a word with which he is not familiar, he "sounds it out". One cannot sound out a word unless he knows the sounds of each alphabetical letter. This should begin, as games, in kindergarten, and should be the first and foremost activity in the first grade. When a child knows ALL the sounds of each letter in the alphabet, then, and only then, can he sufficiently read with comprehension. Other aspects of reading are certainly helpful, such as the look-see method, and helpful situation rules, i.e., "when two vowels go walking, the first on does the talking", etc. Given the irregularity of the English language, sight word teaching is necessary, but without utilizing the phonetic approach first, all other methodology is almost meaningless.

I believe the order of importance in reading competency should be:

1. Recognition of all the small and capital letters of the alphabet.

2. Adequate knowledge of phonetic sounds of all alphabetical letters

3. Mastery of a phonetic approach to learning new words. (Sound it out)

4. Recognition of sight words (grade level)

5. Word comprehension

6. Sentence comprehension (often a child may know the meaning of a word, but has difficulty comprehending the word within the context of a sentence.

7. Paragraph comprehension (what the paragraph tells us)

8. Theme comprehension (what the story is about; how it relates to our knowledge of life so far; how the story makes us feel, etc.)

Of course, in order for a child to learn to read well, he must read often. A teacher should not move forward in lessons until at least ninety percent of the students experience ninety percent success in all of the skills mentioned. When I taught first grade over fifty years ago, each reading group read twice a day. In the morning, while the others did seatwork, each group spent twenty to thirty minutes with me in our little reading corner. A new story was introduced and discussed, new words were learned and their meanings discussed, then the story was read aloud, page by page by each child. In the afternoon, each group re-read the same story, now familiar, so with more ease and proficiency, which in turn, gave each child a sense of accomplishment and success, therefore a sense of reading pleasure. The students also developed better tracking skills, (the speed in which they were able to read) because they were not always in the process of reading new material. Today, this is frowned upon as being redundant and a cause of reading boredom. I disagree. The finest thing a teacher can do for her students is to instill in them a love of reading. Most of us do not enjoy those things we do not do well. I did not know many children adept at reading, who did not enjoy the many books displayed in our reading corner. They enjoyed them because they knew how to read them. Confidence is built upon experience of success, and a child's confidence in his abilities is usually a deciding factor in his learning attitudes.

Some time ago, after having retired from teaching full-time to raise my own children, and before going back to teach full time, I was a substitute teacher for a few years. I subbed in several first grades where reading instruction frequently consisted of only workbook activities. Most first graders read only once a day, and in some of these cases, each child read only a couple of lines. In some first grades, the children read every other day, or just a couple of times a week. Some first grade classes only read aloud as a group. Reading aloud is a worthwhile activity only if practiced in conjunction with a great amount of individual reading, and if led by the teacher at just a slightly faster pace than the students usually read. It improves tracking (the speed at which a child accurately reads) by forcing the readers to move their eyes toward the next word at a more rapid pace than they habitually do. But these particular students assured me that this was their only form of reading instruction. Some of the children in that class did not, themselves, know how they could read alone, and became upset when I asked them to do so.

One day when subbing for a sixth grade teacher, I was interested to note that the children had no reading textbooks. Their teacher had introduced them to ten popular children's fiction books, grade level, which they were to read, then trade with each other throughout the year. Their teacher would then test each student on each book as he or she finished it. I thought the idea was an excellent one for this grade level, until I realized that she didn't teach these students reading skills. The purpose, as I learned from other staff members who also applied this technique in their own classrooms, was to advise the children that "theme" comprehension was the primary importance in reading, with which I primarily agreed. However, as I listened to class members talking among themselves, I discovered that someone would read a book, then tell their friends about the story, so the friends would not have to read that particular book. There were a few in the class who had not read any of the books, and received A's on their tests.

Just to satisfy my own personal curiosity, I chose a book that at least twelve kids had read, picked at random, fifteen words, wrote them on the board, and asked each student to identify each word and define its meaning. Not one person knew all of the words in identity and definition. Seven kids recognized nine of the fifteen words, but did not know the meaning of all nine words. The best results were from four students who knew and defined six of the fifteen words from the book they had just read. Theme knowledge of a story is of utmost value, but without the utilization of reading tools and skills, it is rather like serenading a lover, and not knowing the words to the song.

The type of reading material a child is encouraged to peruse is an important criterion in the advancement of his reading accomplishments. Since the sixties, reading expectations have slipped drastically, and are on a continual decline. There is a decided lack of excellent reading material chosen for students' literature assignments, especially at the junior high and high school level. I am forever thankful for the wonderful English instructor who taught my children in their parochial grade school. Through this marvelous

young man, they experienced the lofty ideals of Sinclair
Lewis, the insightful adventures on the Mississippi told by
Mark Twain, the downtrodden aspects of life in eighteenth
century England as told by Charles Dickens. They enjoyed
the deductive thinking that was applied for solutions for
mystery and intrigue that Arthur Conan Doyle relates.
At the same time, the public schools had geared reading
expectations down to modern children's stories, simple,
enjoyable, fun to read, but definitely not mind reaching.

New books, written for children by recent authors are
fine. Some are very good, in fact. Without ever turning to
them, there would not exist a continuation of knowledge,
contemporary thought, or for that matter, many new
authors. A healthy mixture is necessary, however, and leads
to versatile reading tastes and broader knowledge. There is
an old camp song with these words:

> "Make new friends
> But keep the old.
> One is silver,
> The other is gold."

I believe this philosophy should apply to books and
the type of reading expectations of school students. Most
children of today are totally unfamiliar with names such
as Hawthorne, Thoreau, Longfellow, Emerson. They have
never experienced the wondrous adventures on Treasure
Island, or have empathized with Melville's whaler or his
whale in MOBY DICK. IVANHOE is a truly alien name
to them, and what is more exciting than to ride with Paul
Revere in the middle of the night to warn folks in "every
Middlesex Village and farm?"

The fact is, most teachers of today are equally unfamiliar with such literature. Yet, these are the very types of literature that Robin Williams extolled in the movie, DEAD POET'S SOCIETY. The public raved about the movie, William's role, and what his character proclaimed to be important in reading. The value of the classics is not merely subject matter. It is important to peruse style, historical thought, and imagery produced in good works, to develop a sense of personal, mental, and social growth.

Let me add that children develop a fondness of books and reading, by hearing stories read to them. So, parents, read to your children. Take them to far-away places where they may meet kings and knaves and dragons and princesses. Let them experience adventures and morals set before them on pages of books. Teachers, set aside each day for story time, not only in the primary grades, but in the upper elementary grades as well. Learning activities can be incorporated in stories, such as art projects and writing exercises that help stretch imaginative minds. For, as someone once wrote, "The greatest gift is the passion for reading. It is cheap, it consoles, it distracts, it excites, it gives you knowledge of the world, and an experience of a wide kind. It is a moral illumination."

SPELLING

Another subject that is approached inadequately is spelling. Here again, phonics plays an important role. At least seventy five percent of our English words can be spelled phonetically, and children should be encouraged to do so. But please let us not submit to the new theory that children should be allowed to spell words using their exclusive own phonetic approach. If ever there was an example of "teaching down", this is one. This willy-nilly form of spelling would cause confusion for all of us. As we know, each alphabetical letter has more than one sound, and without a universal agreement on how to spell a word, there would exist no uniformity as to how each of us would sound out a word when reading it. "Don't cik me" may be interpreted as "Don't sik me", or "Don't kike me", depending on whether a person decides to think of the 'c' as soft or hard, and the "I" as short or long. Perhaps used in a sentence, one would come to the conclusion that these words say, "Don't kick me", but why muddy the waters? A person still needs to know phonetic sounds, but common sense needs to prevail here. The English language is confusing enough!

Memory rules, as in reading, are helpful to all of us when we are unsure of a spelling. Rules such as "I before e, except after c, or when sounded like a, as in neighbor or weigh", still occasionally come to my rescue. When I was in university, the experts were beginning to tell future teachers that we should not teach using such memory props, but I believe they are useful to children and adults alike. Of course, some English words must be learned by rote memory because of their inconsistency regarding phonics and memory support rules, but I believe there is not as great an emphasis put on phonics as there should be, although after phonics were completely discarded in the sixties and seventies, and children's reading skills became so poor, phonics have enjoyed a slight resurgence. However, there still is not as great an influence put on proper spelling today, as there was years ago. I remember Friday afternoon spelling bees, and prizewinning bees throughout my entire grade school. One usually doesn't see that today, which is unfortunate because repetition usually promotes proficiency, and spelling is an area in which this is especially true.

WRITING SKILLS

Writing is an art, and like any other artistic endeavor, fundamental basics pertaining to this form of communication must first be learned before creative techniques can be applied.

There is a new approach to writing instruction these days. Witnessed by results, it appears to be counter- productive to good writing skills. It's called 'process writing'. The teacher uses this approach in an attempt to enhance students' desires to write, without expecting proper spelling, sentence structure, or grammar. The child writes his desired theme utilizing no actual writing skills, then he and the teacher discuss proper writing procedures that he should use in his story. Theoretically this method should be a rich learning experience, but too often the child is not expected to go back and apply the proper techniques to eventually produce an accepted piece of literature. Often, in the editing process, the teacher corrects the spelling then and there, and accepts a watered down version of intelligent sentence structure and grammatical correctness in an attempt to retain the child's writing interest. The piece is then published by having the teacher, homeroom mother, or school secretary type it, often making corrections as they do so. The poem or story is fashioned into a book by means of a cover usually made by the student.

The PROCESS of process writing is fantastic! The manner in which it is carried out is usually not. It can be effective in teaching writing skills only if it requires a student to perform in accordance with his grade level abilities and expectations, and if he is required to finalize his work by the use of proper literary skills. Children learn by doing, but first they must be taught. They need to learn how to master specific skills and techniques and use them. They need to be given a chance to learn from mistakes by correcting their own mistakes, using the tools they have learned.

Excellent writers are usually products of excellent writing teachers. A teacher cannot share valuable writing techniques if he, himself, is not expert in this area. Many teachers, fresh from college, are limited in writing skills, so sophisticated sentence structure and vocabulary usage is not demanded of their students. This should not come as a surprise, since many teachers today are products of the seventies and eighties education schemes. (College certifiers, please take note!)

In a letter to "Dear Abby", an American sailor aboard a destroyer in the Persian Gulf, wrote to express his appreciation for mail received from children from all over the world. As grateful as he and his shipmates were, he showed concern over the writing caliber of many American school children. He wrote: "I do not want to appear ungrateful, but what has happened to our school system? I just read a letter from a high school student from a Southwestern state. I quote, 'I now you are doon yore best to pertek our nation fum them and I want you to no we are prowd of you.' The sailor continued his letter, adding: "Abby, this is not unusual, I assure you. I do not know how this student ever got out of the third grade. I just read letters from two foreign students --- one was a Dominican, the other a Russian, ages nine and ten. Their handwriting was very neat and very easy to read, and their spelling was perfect. God help America, if our kids are graduating from high school, writing and spelling the way they do." [24]

SOCIAL STUDIES

The broadest academic school curriculum is social studies. It includes studies in world geography, world history, American history, political science, government, and should also include state and community history. Perhaps teachers have failed our grade school, high school, and college students in this department because the study IS so broad in context; however, I suspect other factors have prevailed that have severely crippled student mastery of understanding in this discipline.

I fear that today, few teachers emerge from their schools of education well versed in historical FACTS and geographic knowledge. If they are informed at all, they are probably receivers of one- sided historical and political views. Most of today's teachers are products of the past five decades of a decidedly left-wing philosophy taught in colleges and universities by left-wing professors. Therefore, grade school and high school teachers arrive in their classrooms only half armed with social studies facts. In many cases, their professors had concentrated on particular "pet" areas of social studies, and the complete factual picture had been sacrificed for the sake of these professors' points of view.

For years I listened to my own college children complain about such cases. My eldest son once had a college professor who, at the beginning of the year, threw out to the students, various political credos, both liberal and conservative, and then asked her students to sit on the side of the room they felt they belonged in terms of political thought, i.e., the liberals on the left, conservatives on the right. My son declared, that after a few weeks in her class, when he compared his thoughts to those of the teacher's, his ideas were so far to the right, he should have been sitting in the hall. The curious aspect of this situation, is the fact that my son was always pretty much a middle of the road thinker, who had never exclusively adhered to a particular political party, nor had he been prone to embrace any extreme political or philosophical ideology.

Another son of mine, who enjoyed a grade point average of 4.0, had a high school teacher, who advised her students that they were selfish and sinful, if they did not believe in community ownership. This woman's entire world history class was devoted to communist theories and Hegelian dialectic thought. Because this young man was an academic striver, he took another history class from another teacher the next semester, so he could learn something.

I was faced with a similar experience when I took post-graduate classes to re-certify my teaching degree, (I had stopped teaching for several years to raise my six children.) I liked and respected my political science professor, and believed him to be an articulate instructor with regard to what he taught. On the first day of class, he explained the far left, the far right, and the middle stance of political thought, and assured us that he intended to cover the entire scope of political thinking. However, our reading material was comprised of left-wing and thoroughly communist material. He encouraged class participation, but each time a student raised a hand to question a point, or make a "middle of the road" or conservative statement, even if the statement was based upon facts, he would say, "That, of course, is what a conservative would say!" If, on the other hand, someone in the class expressed a liberal or left-wing thought, he did NOT respond with," That is what a liberal would say." In most cases, he agreed with the statement. We never delved into far right reading material to counteract the far left material we were assigned.

Most of the students taking the class were young college age people, and had it not been for the few mature individuals who frequently took exception to the way in which super-liberal ideology was presented as absolute and exclusive fact, those young students would never have known other aspects of political thought and persuasions.

We had a guest speaker one evening; a graduate student from the University of Michigan, who had been to Central America. He espoused enormous hatred for Americans and our presence there. He spoke to us as an authoritative figure, yet as various facts were brought to his attention, he became flustered and confused. In one instance, he announced to the class that Fidel Castro's only hope was to create a better life for Cuban people, and he certainly was not a Communist in the true sense of the soviet kind. "In fact," said he, "Castro has never had any association with the Soviet Union." I pointed out to him that Castro was educated in Russia, at Soviet expense. Our speaker declared that he had never heard of such information. Indeed, he probably hadn't. His University of Michigan comrade professors taught him only what they wanted him to know. (I took this class in 1987.)

Such college graduates are going out into the world with little chance of forming solid, personal opinions, based upon broad, conclusive facts. Many of them are teaching our grade school and high school children in this same, distorted, one-sided manner. To my professor's credit, he awarded me an "A" in spite of my many vocal remonstrations in his class. Many students, who complain of biased grading systems, are not so lucky.

Thomas Sowell, an African-American newspaper columnist and articulate author, expressed this viewpoint in one of his articles. "Students who go against the party line can find themselves getting low grades. If not stopped, a whole generation of American college students will hear only what the true believers of the left want them to hear."

Sowell, in the same article, wrote of the difficulty conservative men and women PhDs face with regard to obtaining and keeping teaching jobs. "Recently, a young man studying at a Mid-western college asked me where he could study African history. My suggestion was that he write to Dr. Peter Duignan of the Hover Institution, an internationally recognized scholar specializing in African history. The student did so, and received a reply saying that if he were white and conservative, he should not specialize in African history at all, because there would be no future for him as a college teacher." Sowell added, "Duignan, himself, has never been on the faculty of any college or university, despite his having a PhD and decades of scholarly research and writings that have been highly praised in academic journals. He has dissented from the left-wing views, common among college specialists in African history. It is not just a matter of being white and conservative," Sowell explained. "A black professor of African history at a well known Eastern college did some research in Africa in recent years, and returned with some changed views based on his experiences there. But he has not dared to mention these changes to his colleagues, much less, to his students." (25)

The discouragement of diversified thinking does not take

THE MAKING OF A SECOND WORLD NATION

place with regard to black history alone. It is present in virtually every area of social studies on nearly every campus across these United States of America. It is unfair for students to be fed one-sided views from either side of the political spectrum, and unjust for students to suffer poor grades solely because they express their own opinions, or introduce facts contrary to their professors' political ideologies. It is disingenuous for colleges and universities to hire their teaching staff based upon their left-wing propensities. Don't believe for a moment, that it doesn't happen! Such hiring practices take place with alarming frequency.

A Mrs. Garfield, who holds a degree in classics from England's Cambridge University, was twice rejected for a position at a teaching training college.

Finally, she was granted an interview after pretending to be a left-wing Afro-Caribbean animal rights activist. Mrs. Garfield submitted the false application (under the name of Sharon Shrill) after she believed her legitimate application had been rejected because of her firmly expressed belief in traditional education methods. The bogus application, loaded with grammatical and spelling errors, including two references to "eduction," listed her pastimes as anti-hunting activities, and the radical Animal Liberation Front. Why would a school consider hiring a teacher, who could not spell? "Unfortunately," the dean explained, "It is not unusual that applicants with a degree are not able to spell as well as we would wish." [26]

Where does all of this leave us? It leads us directly to grade school and high school classrooms, just as Marx had envisioned. Our children are learning only half of our historical history. They are not being given several schools of thought. Important events are even being excluded in today's textbooks. The major benefits of learning history are those that identify cause and effect relationships of events that have taken place within the interminable process of evolving civilizations. Most events in human history have shown us that one evil begets a more horrendous evil. In order for future generations to avoid the same pitfalls, and avert the pains of decadence and human destruction in their own lives, serious study must be applied to investigate these mistakes. For instance, the fall of Rome was mainly caused by its gradual moral erosion, to the point that even that extraordinary Republic could not withstand the decadence.

One has to look hard and long to find the nearly non-existent book depicting pre-world Wars I and II Jewish business monopolies throughout the Austro-Hungarian Empire. Yet, there are older German people alive today, who remember begging for stale bread, and being physically kicked into gutters by Jewish merchants and storeowners, and being called "gentile pigs". When I was a child, I remembered hearing a German, who remembered his father being rejected from employment in the business sector because he was a gentile. I remember my father responding with,"I certainly hope folks learn from mistakes in this world, because no one deserves the terrible revenge they are experiencing now."

For centuries, Jews have placed a high value on education and hard work, thus, as a race, they have enjoyed financial success wherever they have lived, which, in turn, has caused unjust jealousies among other peoples. So years of abuse have caused Jewish cultures to adopt a philosophy of defensive exclusiveness, which kindled the fire of anger among non-Jewish European societies. All of this behavior, from both sides, brought about the most hideous atrocities the world had known up to that point in history. All it took was an eloquently speaking madman to fan the flames of discontent during Europe's state of financial depression. He promised change, and boy, did Germany get change! Consider the valuable lessons that could be learned here from both sides. Yet, textbooks only relate Hitler's madness and the awful Holocaust.

The insensitive reign of France brought about the bloody French Revolution. Eighteenth century Czarist Russia so oppressed its citizenry, that the Bolshevik Revolution was embraced and proclaimed by the masses as a saving ideology that was to change their lives. Yet, under Soviet Communist rule, millions of innocent people throughout the world have been enslaved, tortured and killed.

If future generations are not enlightened to mistakes of the past and their terrible repercussions, they will indeed, be condemned to repeat and relive human errors, and in return, suffer the awful consequences. Just look at us today; 2009. We now have people in Washington who have ridden in on eloquent prose speaking promise of "change". They are making new money faster than they did in Germany in the 1930's. They are trying to control every aspect of American life, by presenting such control as "saving us from disaster", while they themselves, live under different standards than the ones they wish to impose upon us. This group of thugs is quietly moving into place, questionable characters, many of whom are self-proclaimed Marxists. And the American people are so complacent and un-aware of what is really going on in their government, they either embrace the fancy double-talk or they do not pay any attention at all.

Since this missive is about our American schools, let's look closely at the man who was chosen by President

Obama to be our SCHOOL SAFETY CZAR. His name is
Kevin Jennings, and he has plans to insist that teachers
include in their social studies lessons, with pro and positive
attitude, the role of cross-dressers, transvestites, gays, etc. in
our society. He has also stated that Harry Hay was one of his
"heroes"; Harry Hay being the man who endorsed MAMBLA,
a sordid group of folks who encourage men to have sex with
young children, as young as eighteen month old babies.
(This information has been taken from the GLEN BECK
SHOW, where Kevin Jennings was actually shown praising
Harry Hay.) This should frighten all decent Americans, but
the truth is, MOST AMERICANS ARE NOT AWARE OF
ANY OF THIS!   And do you want to go back into history?
About fifty years ago, Khrushchev noted that," America will
eventually be a Communist nation, because your people are
so complacent." Do you think?
    Too often, because a teacher is not sufficiently
knowledgeable in her subject, the very definition of social
studies becomes fragmented. In the years between my
full-time teaching, before raising my children and when
I returned to full time teaching, I did a lot of substitute
teaching. On one occasion, I spent three days teaching a
seventh grade social studies class. It was toward the end
of February, when a good portion of their textbook should
have been covered, but this class had not begun to open
their book. I do not advocate exclusive textbook usage,
especially in social studies, but these children had learned
practically nothing about early America, which the seventh
grade in this particular school system covered. The class
was disorderly and unlearned, and lacked self-discipline.
Kids played with window shades, and when asked to stop,
they informed me that their teacher didn't care if they did.

They mostly just walked around the room to chat with one another. Needless to say, I was appalled when they told me that this was what they usually did. Their teacher, they advised me, believed that social studies should teach them to be social, so most of their days were spent socializing with each other. The principal concurred with that assessment, without any disapproval. Should we wonder why our school children are deficient in social studies, or why our young and not-so-young adults today are ready to buy into any political rhetoric someone throws at them in the guise of "taking care" of them? If the American people knew their history, they would not be so eager to be "taken care of."

Many classes, parading under the auspicious title of social studies, delve into realms that should be considered nothing more than fad programs. Death education, sex education, and other "social" considerations are more often than not, taught sans morals. Many of these so-called "emotional health " programs such as health education, drug prevention, values- clarification, and situation ethics do little to improve a child's wholesome outlook toward himself and his life. In fact, these studies often tend to bring undesirable facets of living into focus, when they would not have been contemplated before the child took the class. New studies have come to light to indicate that more young people commit suicide after taking suicide prevention classes than those who are involved with parents and teachers who quietly and simply hold that this awful measure of finality is unacceptable problem solving; not worth discussing, and certainly not worth consideration.

To believe children should take a class such as suicide prevention, is to assume that those children are apt to, or are at least capable of, performing such an inane act. It is far wiser to show a child respect by letting him know that you think he is far too wise to resort to such behavior. I cannot imagine myself sitting down with my own children to discuss reasons why they should not kill themselves, any more than I can imagine listing reasons why it would be unwise for them to commit murder. I'm certain they would take it as an insult to their reasonable sensibilities. They would be justified in their views.

Ask yourself- then be honest in your answer. Would it enhance your self-respect and self-esteem, if someone were to sit down with you to discuss why you should not take your own life in the face of life's tribulations, or would you feel that person does not possess the faith in you that you deserve? Also, would it blot out the possibility of considering such action, or bring into focus the possibility of electing to pursue that terrible option? There are some areas of thought that should be taken for granted as unacceptable, and in deference to individuals with whom one is dealing, an assumption should be shown that you believe them to be above approach in this matter. If a person shows signs of mental and or emotional disturbance, and seems to be at risk to himself or others, he should be cared for in a loving and professional manner. This should be done on an individual basis, not as an "across the board" curriculum.

Sex education has not deterred promiscuous sexual behavior, mainly because it is taught as an activity in which to take precautions, not as something to avoid until marriage. It seems ludicrous, that in public schools where God must never be mentioned, and prayer is forbidden, the use of condoms for premarital sex is introduced and encouraged, and even in some schools, passed out to the students. For the sake of future America, social studies subjects must be selected with prudence and decent taste, and with the moral good of individuals and society in mind. It must be taught in an accurate and stimulating and interesting manner. And it must be taught utilizing historical FACTS.

We are parts of history; a story unfolding with ups, downs, good and bad. Geography is not merely a study of maps. Geography is knowing where a place is located in the world, why certain cultures in certain lands possess their unique characteristics, and the historical, agricultural, and industrial components that have played a part in the shaping of mores' in such civilizations. Exciting things can take place in a social studies classroom, but in order for this to happen, a teacher must be well informed, and excited about her subject, and be able to share her expertise in an articulate and interesting manner. And, ALWAYS, a teacher must expect academic effort from her students. Before any American can intelligently evaluate future progress, he must first know what has taken place before his time in his nation and in his world.

MATH AND SCIENCE

The disciplines of math and science are so vital to world competition in such various areas of technology that the bottom line is, the country that excels in these areas, is the country that excels in world influence and authority. Yet less than six percent of American university students majored in either of these subjects in the nineties. [27] Guess what! The same holds true today. You won't see many recent bibliographies in the back of this book, because not much has changed! This is not to say that most grade school children lack the proclivity to delve into science and math related subjects. Science has always held a high interest among young children, and math, if presented with élan, would also be received with enthusiasm. But do to the lack of grade school and high school teachers who are prodigious in these disciplines, children are not encouraged to embrace these subjects in their higher learning years, so they do not become priorities in their academic achievements.

The subjects of math and science are not being presented to high school students by enthusiastic educators, and minimal knowledge is required in most classrooms. If a subject is approached with high interest attitudes from the teacher, with high expectations of top-notch performance from the students, I believe the derived sense of academic achievement and accomplishment will spur more college-bound students to focus on these categories of learning. When a person becomes extraordinarily knowledgeable in a subject, he frequently develops an interest in that subject, and becomes motivated to search for deeper insights. Again, study, application, and homework are needed for this to happen. Teachers must expect this effort if we are to generate a greater number of scientific and mathematically inclined college-bound students to major and excel in these technologically important areas.

ENGLISH AND LITERATURE

The English studies department is another that encompasses a wide scope of learning. Grammar, sentence structure, composition, literature, and writing techniques are main components within this category. Most of these skills can, and should be used in conjunction with nearly every other school subject, but all too often, they are not. The question should be asked, "Why not?"

Few people today emerge from high schools, even colleges, with sufficient adeptness with which to express themselves. Vocabulary usage has been geared down to such a degree that I fear another few decades will find that folks will be left with little more than simulated grunts, accompanied with one word sentences. I believe that word usage has become limited over the past forty or fifty years in conjunction with the lack of classical reading that has taken place in schools and homes. We experience the beauty of language when we read well- written poetry or prose. The problem is that very few teachers today are well-read people, so they don't encourage sophisticated vocabulary usage of their students. Thus, today's school children are failing to learn and utilize the many tools we have at out disposal with which to express ourselves. What a pity!

As a history teacher, I often assigned theme essays. As I mentioned in an earlier chapter, I found the writing proficiency of my kids sorely lacking in punctuation. I used to tell them to read their work out loud, breathing as they had punctuated it. If some of them had obeyed me to the letter, we would have had to order oxygen in for them. The rewarding part of this for myself, and for my students, was the immense improvement they showed as the year progressed. Plus, we had a lot of laughs and fun while they were improving.

It is interesting to note probable causes of our decline in writing excellence. In years past, writing was the only form of communication between persons who geographically were unable to communicate orally. With the introduction of the telephone, the need to communicate and keep in touch with each other through writing diminished. One could simply dial the phone to convey a thought or relay a message. The onset of various modes of transportation made it possible for friends, family, and business associates to see each other more often. Thus, the art of letter writing ceased to be necessary. In most cases today, letters are written as pleasurable means for keeping in touch with loved ones on an infrequent basis, or as business correspondence.

It is also interesting to note how the emergence of the computer world, and advanced technology has influenced our writing habits. Texting is a whole other language; I, myself, cannot read it or understand it, but it works just fine for my grandkids, and my adult children. My very bright eighteen-year-old grandson had trouble reading a sentiment I wrote to him on his birthday card, because it was written in cursive. So times are changing, folks, and technology is moving faster than some of us can keep up. I still believe the need to express oneself in an articulate manner is vitally important, and teachers should do their best to see that these skills are taught.

THE ARTS

It is similarly disappointing to note the lack of following and appreciation for the arts. Since the beginning of the thirties, interest in the classics found in fields of music, dance, sculpture, painting, etc., has diminished, and has been replaced with an over-riding zeal for modern, "pop" artistic endeavors, which, in turn, has diminished the "class" in classical art. Perhaps this has been the cause of our society to become crass and crude, or the fact that our society has become crass and crude has caused the arts to become so.

The entertainment world has been reduced to hard-core mediocrity, and as long as people accept this change for the worse, it will continue to go downhill in depth and substance. Several years ago, in an interview on television, a movie producer claimed that, "There are millions of garbage eaters out there, and as long as people continue to like garbage, I will continue to produce cheap, garbage movies." Apparently not many people were insulted by this proclamation; the garbage eaters have grown to alarmingly high numbers, willing to patronize, and therefore financially support low-grade entertainment. Imagine what we would get if everyone refused to patronize "R" rated movies, even those which are well written and produced? Perhaps the caliber of movies would rise to meet the demands of the public. The "R" content would be deleted from the superior ones; the substandard others would be discontinued altogether, thereby promoting a sense of decency in their scripts while maintaining their superior productions. I admit that there are a few (very few) movies that, in order to validate the subject content, there must be some sensitive scenes interspersed throughout the movie. I understand that. But, I am also willing to say that this is not as frequently necessary as the modern producers profess.

There is a decided lack of moral message in most forms of entertainment, including the fields of painting and sculpture. Many of these forms of entertainment not only condone, but also encourage immoral behavior as accepted social decorum. Is it any wonder that nearly six of every ten teenagers have premarital sex, often with multiple partners, and nearly five of every ten unmarried girls become pregnant before their twenty- first birthday? Should we be surprised that preteen and teen drug abuse is at epidemic proportions, and sexual abuse has been continually on the rise over the past several decades? Isn't it time to address the fact that divorce, spouse abuse, family and community violence, and sexually transmitted diseases are major causes of the breakdown of our society? If one's senses are exquisitely enhanced by a resplendent sunset, it stands to reason that violent, repugnant scenes displayed before us on television or movie screens affect us in a socially and morally negative way.

The main reason why children are virtually without values, is that they haven't been taught acceptable values. They have not been taught by their parents, their churches, or their schools. They haven't been taught by example or word. And in most cases today, parents and teachers were not tutored on the importance of values such as honesty, moral integrity and principles. Children are not the only "garbage eaters" in our culture. Their parents and teachers endorse amorality, and in turn, convey the erroneous message that morality in a society is not necessary for a person's well being. So today, the rapes, robberies, murders, drug addiction, emotional and physical domestic abuse continue to rage throughout our American culture like uncontrollable diseases.

It is inane to suppose that liberal arts will, by themselves, lead us out of this spiritual morass, but I firmly believe that this academic area is a good starting point. I remember, as a rebellious teen-ager, I once asked my mother why anyone would want to sit through a symphony, and she replied, "Because it's a civilized thing to do. It soothes and refines the soul."

We have become an unrefined society, and as the broad definition of unrefined is crude, I further declare that we have become crude.   Colleges and universities have not required students to possess sufficient knowledge of the humanities for the past several decades; therefore students in most American schools have not been introduced to, and taught to appreciate the higher elements of esthetic thinking.   Colleges have become training schools rather than places of intellectual enlightenment. As a result, grade school and high school students have lacked the teachers to tutor them in liberal arts.

There are many ways in which art enriches people's souls, and encourages them to soar to higher planes in life. Great authors of great books, great plays written and produced by gifted writers, beautiful sculptures and paintings created by the hands of talented artists enable us to experience lofty imaginings.   Teachers and parents need to advance the thinking process of the next generation of Americans. We CAN rise from our present philistine mentality to a higher ground of philosophical logic. The ancient, and not so ancient teachers of the world shared valuable insights for us to utilize. We have been given great cornerstones with which to build principled lives of social wisdom. Rather than push them into obscurity and forget them, let us build upon the old, while continuing onward to higher goals and aspirations.

EVALUATION OF TEACHERS

Classroom attitudes should be an extension of desirable home attitudes. This necessitates the teacher to be a morally positive example to her students. I have sat in teachers' lounges where the language was so crude, one might think the speakers were from a reform school, rather than from colleges of education. If one habitually speaks with obscenities, it stands to reason that he also thinks in obscenities. Teachers, along with the rest of our society, have lapsed into a moral morass. They have compromised high principles in favor of popular tastes. Since they have not learned a great deal of cultural distinctions, they are no more aware than the uneducated populace, of the immediate and gradual consequences felt from compromised values within a society. It is of vital importance that the adults who preside over our kids at least six hours each week day, possess the same qualities of honest, moral integrity that are necessary for our children.

I believe the screening processes that are required for both school system and college personnel do not place adequate emphasis on this issue. Colleges and universities seem to be concerned exclusively with prescribed credit hours when awarding their students certification to teach in American schools, and school personnel administrators place too much emphasis on whether the prospective teacher is an advocate of neo-modern teaching methods, which as evidenced by modern academic results, are not very effective.

Teachers, more than any professional group, cannot afford to be lax in any area of deportment. Their entire career constitutes values set by example. Their job not only involves advocating academic excellence of their students, but it must also promote social virtues as well.

I do not mean to say that all teachers are without moral and ethical standards. I have taught with many men and women, who have possessed wonderful attributes of fine human beings. However, there are as many teachers in our school systems who, in my opinion, do not meet the ethical and moral requirements necessary for the personification of excellent classroom examples. The teaching profession is unlike any other occupation. Like parents, teachers deal with the awesome responsibility of shaping future adult Americans, who in turn, will some day be the decision makers of our nation. This endeavor should never be taken lightly.

As an extension of home support, teachers must continue to generate feelings of self-respect and self-esteem in their students, and as always, this should be accompanied with expectations of self-discipline and personal responsibility on the part of the students. To achieve this, a spirit of cheerful and positive decorum should reign in the classroom, just as it should in the home. If a child FEELS that he can learn, he is usually ABLE to learn to his potential, for a positive approach helps a child to allow his mind to be open to learning and knowledge. His feeling of well-being allows him to broaden his focus toward the subject at hand. A show of respect for each child's feelings enables a child to in turn, feel respect for his teacher, thereby generating a mutually healthy relationship between the learned and the learning. So therefore, if a teacher is consistent, fair and just, the imperative demands of academic and behavioral excellence will not be so difficult to attain.

All modes of teaching should be utilized daily, because different children learn with different tools, while using their unique mental capacities. Some children learn best by kinesthetic means, some by visual means, while some comprehend and process knowledge best with an audio mode of presentation. It is important for a teacher to be aware of this, and present her subject accordingly, using ALL methods for each subject.

An extremely important criterion for good teaching is extensive knowledge of subject matter on the part of the teacher. As I have already mentioned, this is oft-times lacking in the teaching profession today. Also mentioned earlier, is the fact that most of us enjoy doing that which we do well. This is true of teachers, as well as students. A teacher who knows and loves her subject, will transmit that exuberance to her students. The more knowledge a teacher possesses, the more knowledge can be shared with students.

While it is true that a teacher needs to be an expert in her field in order to teach well, an expert in an academic discipline is not always a good teacher. I hear numerous reports from young people, especially at the high school and college level, of teachers and professors who are brilliant in their fields, but do not possess the ability to explain the subject material in a clear, articulate manner. If a principal or college dean notices that unusually large portions of students fail, or consistently receive low marks under the tutelage of a certain teacher or professor, while those same students perform well in other classes, his teaching ability should be more thoroughly investigated. Sometimes, in cases of foreign teachers, poor diction, or the inability to speak the English language adequately is a drawback to student comprehension. This particular problem is an on-going complaint with many high school and college students. Personnel must consider these factors during hiring procedures.

It is unfair to students to expect them to comprehend subject matter if they cannot interpret what the teacher is saying. There are many cases at the college level where students simply cannot understand the teacher. In some cases, the teacher, when told that he is not communicating well orally, will write his information on the blackboard. Good idea, except that in most cases, the teacher's writing is so illegible, the students cannot read it. This type of situation is commonplace in most universities, yet nothing seems to be done about it. More and more foreign teachers and professors are being hired each year without their pronunciation being taken into account, and more and more students are being put at a distinct disadvantage.

In addition to being well versed in subject matter, and being able to present that subject matter in a clear and comprehensive fashion, it is necessary for a teacher to be aware of the emotional, mental and psychological capacities of her students with regard to attention span, comprehensive language, and social interaction of each chronological age grouping. In every grade and subject, utmost effort should be given to find a child's academic comfort zone, then help him to travel beyond that to his maximum comprehensive ability to reach a higher-level comfort zone. This requires the teacher to walk a very fine line to ensure that she is not being too easy, yet not setting the child up for failure by expecting more than his capabilities can handle.

A person generally learns best by doing. I firmly believe that college students who major in the field of education, should student teach half of their junior year, and half of their senior year. I think this is starting to happen in many universities today, and it is a good thing. In addition, I feel that, upon graduation, she should co-teach for a full year before being awarded her own classroom. If not that, she should be required to be a substitute teacher for a full year. I can assure you, much can be learned about good and poor teaching procedures in one year of substituting; enough to properly prepare a teacher for a successful career of her own. Such an experience also prepares a teacher for myriad situations that are apt to arise throughout a teacher's career. There is a saying, "If it doesn't happen when you're substitute teaching, it probably has never happened." Being a substitute teacher also provides opportunities to borrow nifty ideas from other good teachers, so one is able to amass a collection of methods and techniques, and observe how they relate to students and their studies. All-in all, I believe that once a person has been a substitute teacher for a year, he or she will be far better equipped to deal with all aspects of being a really good teacher in his or her own classroom.

It is up to colleges and universities across this nation to ensure that their graduated teachers leave their institutions equipped with proper and adequate skills and knowledge. I have often been appalled at the frequency of poor grammar and limited intelligence that some teachers have displayed. While substitute teaching, I've had notes left for me by the absent teacher, such as,"I hope you're day is good" and "Charles have to make up his test." and "He don't listen very good, so watch him." Poor grammar and poor vocabulary usage is inexcusable in those who are being paid to teach such skills. It is the vital responsibility of professors and state certifiers to send out well-rounded, logical thinkers; rich in subject knowledge and the humanities, for the combination is what lifts a person to higher planes of thought, and enables him to share greater depth and scope of thought. Being a teacher, like being a parent, is an awesome, delicate, and complex responsibility. It is also more rewarding than almost any other occupation or endeavor.

An effective way to ensure that teachers are ready to leave their higher learning institutions, and present themselves to classroom students as viable, learned and skilled educators, is to administer effective, determining evaluation tests that adequately demonstrate the extent of their knowledge and skills, as well as their personal character traits. This necessitates college and university certifiers to up-grade their OWN standards of expectations. It also requires teachers who teach teachers to scrutinize present and past tenets of educational philosophies to discover what old and new ideologies have proven to be effective, and which ones have not worked. Again, change does not always promote improvement. Sometimes returning to methods and attitudes of the past, when children DID learn, promotes greater progress.

EVALUATION OF STUDENTS

The testing that is done in grade schools and high schools must also be addressed and re-evaluated. Too many different schools within various school systems administer diverse tests that fluctuate drastically in terms of difficulty. Quite often, a child attending a parochial school, is subjected to far more intricate and thorough evaluation of subject matter than his public school peers. A child earning an A or B in one school would fail if tested in another school. The "dumbing down" of tests does not ultimately help anyone; it merely expects less of a child, thus limiting the potential performance of which that child is capable. After all, we are all human beings who perform according to what we are EXPECTED to do, not what we are ABLE to do.

Types of testing are as important as standards of difficulty within tests. We have become a nation of "multiple choice", yet actual knowledge of an academic subject is not consistently demonstrated in a multiple-choice test. Too often, this form of evaluation becomes a "multiple guess" exercise, or at best, a test given with clues. Frequently it simply demonstrates a person's ability to successfully take a multiple choice type test. Admittedly, some logical thinking is evidenced in such a case, but it does not necessarily encompass logical

112

thinking with regard to the specific subject matter.

Some teachers actually design tests so as to trick their students, by inserting confusing verbiage into the A-B-C choices. Why they do this is beyond my comprehension. It is clearly unproductive in the teaching and learning of a subject, and does not evaluate adequately, what the students have or have not learned about that subject. I rather think that this action on the part of the teacher has more to do with the teacher's ego, than his or her desire to truly evaluate her students' knowledge.

Often, teachers administer multiple-choice tests, because they are quicker, and easier to grade. The high school, in which I taught social studies, had a wonderful, computerized machine that corrected multiple-choice tests in a matter of seconds. I believe I was the only teacher who insisted on administering tests that required students to fill in the blanks, complete the sentences, or answer the question in essay form. I was a harder task-maker of myself, because I believed that test results indicated my own teaching ability, as well as my students' knowledge of the subject which I had been teaching them.

I believe tests of scholastic ability should be administered throughout a child's school years. For the most part, this is already done throughout the United States, but not enough attention is being done about the results of this testing. No child should proceed to the next step in his education if he is unable to master subject matter expected of him thus far. Therefore, testing should be carried out at the end of each school year for every grade to determine whether or not they are ready for the next grade. By the time a child reaches the eighth grade, he or she would not be terribly off the mark in preparation for high school. High school is such a milestone in a child's life, that it's paramount that he is sufficiently ready for that new venture. All of these testing procedures should be standardized, providing a national assessment system of evaluation throughout a child's school years. Most important, national standardized tests should be given to high school seniors before they are given graduation diplomas. It is imperative that a common sense code of expectations prevails throughout our nation, for although we are a group of United States, we are also one nation, and it is our nation's children for whom we must be concerned. If America is to keep pace with the worldwide information revolution, we must solve the problems of our nation's intellectual and mental development, and we must employ sound, adequate testing procedures to do this. The "dumbing down" of tests and textbooks will not solve the problems of today's poor scholastic performance, as has recently been observed in our nation's children and young adults.

It is true that not all high school graduates have the mental skills or desire to attend college. There are myriad higher learning institutions which can further a person's capacity to succeed in today's world. If a student is not emotionally or academically ready for college, he may choose a technical trade school or a career training school. There are many that supply sufficient knowledge for success in various fields such as electronics, computer-aided drafting, automobile mechanics, business secretarial skills, and medical personnel skills, to name a few.

I feel the need here, to caution such interested students. The philosophy of the corporation heads of many of these schools is less than magnanimous. They are out to make money, pure and simple, which is the American way, but some are none too principled as to how they attain their financial profits.   For over three years, I worked as an admissions representative for a technical career training school, and in thirty- nine months, I witnessed twenty nine reps. hired and fired because they did not meet their enrollment "quotas". The school in which I worked demanded that each rep. enroll twelve students per month, or termination would take place. Needless to say, in order to keep their jobs, some of the admission representatives resorted to embellishing features of the school to the point of out-right lying to the prospective student. The directors did not mind this, and turned a blind eye to this because the bottom-line; in fact, in some of these schools, the ONLY line, was the profit line.

Many of these career schools are very expensive, and prospective students had better be prepared to study hard in order to perform well in classes to ensure that a good job will be there upon completion. The loans necessary to pay for such schooling and training can be financially ruinous if a graduate cannot be rewarded with a job. Since some of the students in the less responsible institutions are accepted if they pass the "mirror test", and show no more thinking power than that, the school eventually earns a poor reputation as graduating poorly trained people who have not performed well in the business sector upon graduation.   As a result, many of these training schools have been forced by their state, to close their doors due to high loan default percentages.

The up side of career training schools, the good ones, is that most of them have good placement services. When choosing a career training school, call several companies that hire people with your intended job description. If several companies respond favorably by expressing satisfaction with graduates they have hired from that particular school, indications are that the school is probably a reputable and good school.

Today's high emphasis on technical skills provides jobs for graduates of technical training as often, if not more often, than for college graduates who lack specific skills. The knowledge learned at these trade schools, at least gets graduates in the door of a good company. If a person wishes to go on to higher learning at the college level, he or she is at least making sufficient money to afford that objective. Often, companies will offer financial help to valued employees so they can advance their education.

I see nothing wrong with installing a format of testing for high school seniors, which would offer a choice of two tests; one for college-bound students, and one for those not interested in going to college. Both tests must be solid, adequate forms of evaluating scholastic skills and development necessary for high school graduation, and must show required mental performance of the person taking the test. By giving the graduating student a choice, institutions dealing with high school graduates can improve their own programs and expectations. Seniors, who do not wish to attend college, will have a better view of their own capabilities without feeling the pressure of college preparatory advancement testing.

This should not place any high school senior in a permanent category, whereby he or she could never seek a college education. There should always be college entrance tests given to whoever desires a college education. Often times, a high school senior is not mature enough nor motivated enough to yearn for collegiate studies at the time of his graduation, but changes his mind a few years down the road. I do believe, however, this dual form of testing high school seniors would greatly benefit the graduates in terms of choices; the college-bound, in their choice of colleges, and perhaps, even in choosing a major, and the employment-seeking graduate in the choice of job placement. It would also benefit the business sector in cities and towns across our country, for these tests would naturally indicate the variety and types of skills in which a person excels, thus expediting the graduate's procurement of fulfilling employment.

Numerous businesses are now endorsing plans to assess high school and college graduates' skills, by linking basic and selective fields of endeavor to demonstrated knowledge and skill level. Business leaders can also help in the formulation of undergraduate studies, by advising school systems as to various skills employers need in conjunction with the variety of job descriptions within specific companies. Corporations are discovering what they term a "skills gap" between the abilities of high school graduates, and the needs of an increasingly technical work place. In 1988, (then) U.S. Secretary of Labor, Elizabeth Dole began to create a commission of business and industry needs to stay competitive in the world market place, and that workers need to cope with new technologies. "Simply put," stated Mrs. Dole, "America's work force is in a state of unreadiness." [28]

John Bishop, associate professor at Cornell University's school of industrial and labor relations in the eighties, (and may still be there) opined that the "gap" reflects the fact that American students, in contrast to those in Western Europe, lack an incentive to work any harder in high school, than the minimum amount needed to earn a diploma. "In the United Kingdom, Ireland, France, and Italy," he noted, "Students take a battery of exams .How well they do is a critical determinant in whether they get a job. They have a strong incentive to work hard in high school." Mr. Bishop added that, "Unlike firms in Europe, American companies tend to hire youths out of high school for high paying, career oriented jobs in the so-called primary job market." [29]

If more corporations were to form partnership alliances with educators to determine performance skills of graduating seniors, many job opportunities could open up for youths, by allowing employers to find skilled graduates they might otherwise not know about. Thus, they could pay them according to their individual level of expertise. High school students would also have a better idea of skills that will be required of them when they enter the job market. Hopefully, they would then be more motivated to excel in those skills. The world is continually changing with regard to technological advancements, and it is vitally important that student readiness to cope with technology is constantly addressed and updated. We need good teachers to do this.

Part III

THE FREEDOM OF CHOICE

If children need incentive to work harder to achieve satisfactory results, teachers, being made of the same human predilections, also require incentive to encourage exemplary performance. Merit pay, and the abolishment of teacher tenure have become popular answers to solutions of public school teaching and learning inadequacies. I agree with this idea. There is no reason why a consistently effective teacher should NEED tenure, and there is no reason why a poor teacher should HAVE it. Too often, once persons receive the security of tenure, they relax their efforts and tend to settle back comfortably into an uncreative, non-innovative, perfunctory mode of teaching. Teachers have virtually nothing to fear, once they are protected by tenure, for it is nearly impossible to rid a school system or university of a bad, ineffective or immoral classroom teacher. As for merit pay; what is wrong or unfair about paying a person according to his or her performance? The ultimate academic achievement of students is the purpose of a teacher's career.

How do we ensure that our children are being taught to attain their scholastic and personal best? The answer lies in the area of competitiveness. Along with individual teacher merit pay, I firmly believe that schools should be able to be patronized according to their ability to turn out culturally and academically sound students. It has been pointed out time and again, money is not the primary deciding factor in effective teaching. Private and parochial schools have for years, been havens of excellent teaching and productive learning. This is because most private and parochial schools, and most of the parents who send their children to them, encourage and demand the very traits I have mentioned as necessary tools for academic and personal achievement, and most of these schools are run on the proverbial shoestring.

Unfortunately, not everyone can afford to send his or her children to private schools. This leads us to the consideration of parental "freedom to pursue happiness" for themselves and their children. As we all know, America was founded upon the constitutional rights of liberty and freedom for all. This principle must include the freedom of choice, be it choice of church, speech or school. We, as citizens of America, under due process of the laws of our constitution, possess the right to work toward the pursuit of happiness in the form of whatever lawful life we wish, which naturally involves lawful means of acquiring desired lifestyles. Education is beyond a doubt, the most powerful and practical means with which to attain intellectual growth and scholastic success. It goes without saying; deeper knowledge generally precipitates our ability to pursue happiness.

There have been many ideas voiced about the manner in which to bring this concept to fruition. The freedom of choice could be carried out in a variety of phases and designs, but some major factors must be part of the plan. First of all, it must include both private and public learning institutions. The total sphere of public school effectiveness is held in question today; therefore the entire education system is in need restructuring and improvement. If choice were exclusive to only public schools, it would leave us with competition between schools owned by the same bureaucratic government. Public schools that can keep their same market share over areas of districts are not likely to change very much. No matter what schools parents choose for their children, the same state mandates, the same teachers' union, and the same tenure would prevail, which would leave us with the same bureaucratic and personnel control that would ultimately suffocate reform and would preclude any improvement in academic performance.

Educational choice must cross the lines of districts as well. Allowing parents to choose their schools wherever they wish leads to ultimate accountability of teaching and learning institutions. There would be no monopoly on the children who live within their district, and no monopoly could run any educational system, given that the private sector is included in the "choice" plan. Students from low-income families would not be trapped in low- income schools. Wealthy people could leave an ineffective district, and enroll their children in another district.

Critics of this plan argue that poor and minority students would feel disoriented in a school atypical of their past school environment. I disagree. It has been discovered, where some choice has been in effect, such as Massachusetts and Minnesota, children have academically and personally thrived. It has attracted hundreds of dropouts back into classrooms voluntarily. Scholastic ability often transcends beyond socio-economic neighborhoods and suburbs. Most parents are concerned about the quality of education for their children, and their safety while their children are housed within the walls of their school more than they are about racial or social isolation.

Parents and their children should have the freedom to choose the kind of school that best fits their individual needs and sociological tastes. These special interests should naturally include such aspects as discipline philosophy, achievement standards, social and moral ideals, extent of curriculum, methods of instruction, social interaction between students and teachers, and social interaction between the students, themselves. In other words, different types of parents and children should, and would, have a variety of school environments from which to choose.

Each school should be operated autonomously; each deciding its type of teaching staff and textbooks, which academic disciplines it intends to offer, and its own student expectation guidelines. Thus, each school would develop a reputation for possessing its own unique character. It has been proposed by some, that the teacher within each school "business" could own a part of their learning institution. This would free teachers from bureaucratic demands and restraints, to teach according to their own designs, talents, and personally preferred techniques. Principals, (or presidents) of each school would naturally choose teachers who are in accord with their own philosophical dispositions. The professionalism of teachers would be put into a clear focus of what it really is; an honorable profession, which if applied and treated with prudence and rectitude, may result in strong leadership, clear goals, ambitious, academic programs, and innovative teaching practices. In fact, research data has shown that teacher morale is higher in schools of choice than in today's traditional schools.

I suggest that each school have its own counseling

services to aid parents and children in their decisions. Some regulations would need to be enforced in this area. These counselors must not be "sales" people, whose salaries are paid by, or whose job security is dependent upon the number of students they attract and enroll in school. This is where some propriety schools have become disreputable. It would naturally be to the school's benefit if honesty were to prevail in such counseling, for in the end, one of two situations would come to exist. One, the parents and students would be delighted with their choice of school if the school is in agreement with the needs and goals of the students. In this case, since parents, students, and teachers will all feel in accord with one another, and will all have a voice and play a part in the education of the students, a sense of well-being and pride will be felt by all involved. I believe that in this type of scenario, vandalism, truancy, discipline problems, and parental lassitude will decrease. Drop out rates have already abated in schools of choice, and those are choices involving just public schools within certain area limits. When everyone concerned is empowered in the decision making for the good of the student, it stands to reason that those very persons involved, will develop a high interest in the entire academic arena. Unification of principles between parents, teachers, and students will also bring about solid home relationships so needed in today's world.

On the other hand, if the counseling and information given to parents and their children presents a false picture of the real character and environment of the school, parents and children will soon become disenchanted with the school, its teachers, its principal, and principles, and quickly transfer to another school. Included in the criteria and regulations involved within this plan, shall be the ability of the student to transfer at any time without financial penalty. If principals and their teachers have a financial stake in their business of education, they will not be happy to lose student enrollment. Since each school will be paid for each warm body it shelters, principals and their teaching staff will need to be competitive with other schools. This, of course, will result in improvement and excellence in our education institutions. Schools will either become more responsive to consumers, parents and students, or expire.

All of this can be precipitated with the implementation of the voucher system, similar to that of the old G.I. bill. This would take the money for the education of children out of the hands of distant bureaucrats, and place it into the rightful hands of parents. Parents would simply be given a set amount of money in the form of a voucher to be redeemed at the school of their choice. This amount should be determined by cost amount analysis of yearly expenditures necessary per pupil, spread evenly across the entire country. It is my guess that when education bonds are proposed in election years, parents will more readily respond in a positive manner, since they will be more satisfied with their children's education program. The appropriation per pupil would go directly to the family, deeming it unnecessary to pay bureaucrats their share for management purposes, which today encompasses a high cost governmental machine. Also, there would be no spending gap between the rich and the poor, bringing the ideal of educational equality, designed by our forefathers, into reality. There would also be no reason to make excuses for folks who yell "racism", or "poverty", or any other means with which to excuse poor behavior or poor effort on the part of the children. There would be a uniform amount of money spent on each student, no matter where they attend school.

Under the freedom of choice system, there would be a need for limited regulation guidelines in terms of constitutional rights, national scholastic and sociological standards. Teacher certification must remain in order for the profession to be protected, and for professionalism to reign within school businesses. Every profession today, i.e., dental, medical, law, etc., is protected by an association requiring respective degrees, and this should apply to the teaching profession as well. Specific guidelines and testing of teachers, as has already been mentioned, are necessary to ensure that each educator has established proficiency in subject knowledge, and possesses the ability to comprehensively teach his or her subject.

Since each school must be free to function autonomously, each must be responsible for its own transportation system. Of course, some may choose to not provide any form of transportation for their students; this would be a factor in parental decisions in choosing a school with or without transportation. It is important to remember that parents will now be consumers, and in most cases, if consumers believe they are paying more than services are worth, they look elsewhere. But transportation or no transportation, busses or no busses, there will be a need for some sort of state or national regulations concerning safety standards.

National testing at various grade levels will be a fundamental determining factor in the success of any school. The results of such tests must allow for variables such as individual student I.Q., emotional detriments and capacities, etc. Eventually, those places where children learn best will thrive and grow. Those that fail to produce adequate results will be shunned, and it will not take many years before their doors will be closed.

Freedom of choice in education will indeed, benefit our nation, and bring it back to being a first rate, first world nation intellectually, technologically, and industrially. Competition generates better productivity in the business world, and it will do so in the academic world. Excellent teachers can charge and be paid accordingly; poor teachers will no longer be in demand. I can think of no better incentive to become an effective teacher. The hard part of all of this will be to wrest control from the bureaucrats, and place it where it belongs; in the hands of parents throughout the country. With enough support from the voting public, I hope it can be done. Monies for the education of our youth must be placed where it belongs—with those most interested in the general welfare of children—their parents.

SUMMARY

have described a utopian scenario; a basic, fundamentally sound utilization of appropriate decorum in the home and in the classroom. I have described a restoration of values and high expectations commensurate with the regeneration of our American children's personal and scholastic achievement and growth. It is not an impossible dream. Every solution, every example, every suggestion is simple, workable, and entirely plausible. Such ideals will bring joy and peace and harmony into the home, brought about by genuine love, caring, commitment, high personal expectations and mutual respect toward all family members. Warm laughter can replace harsh words. Tenderness can replace physical abuse. Children's respect for adults and adults' respect for their children can generate a mutual respect and deep regard for all mankind. It will spill over into classrooms where high regard is given to others; where accountability is accepted and expected of self, and where social, moral, and scholastic strivers are admired. Oh, to think of it! It is all so readily within our reach.

Until Americans are willing to accept these simple challenges, let me share a word of warning with you young college graduates who are in pursuit of a teaching career. Do not venture to espouse the ideas written on these pages, or ever indicate in your interview with any prospective school superintendent, that you believe in firm discipline and high academic standards. You won't be hired. Never state that you consider phonics to be a primary concern in teaching children to read. You won't be hired. And never applaud old- fashioned values as necessary tools one must possess in order to teach and learn effectively. You will not be hired. If you hint that perhaps children's modern behavioral liberation has resulted in their not learning, you will be contemptuously viewed as obsolescent and inept, and you will not be hired.

Instead, disclose your knowledge of the so-called new methodologies and modern philosophies of education. Reflect on the idea that new teaching concepts are always the best avenues to take, regardless whether children actually learn from their applications, and you will have better than reasonable chances of teaching in any public school district. It should please you to know that your lack of experience is to your advantage. More mature teachers have too many tried and true insights up their sleeves to be considered competent teachers.

I wish you luck in your endeavors. I know that most of you truly aspire to be fine teachers, and many of you will reach that goal, in spite of the incredible detriments you will face. I ardently hope you will have the good sense to reflect upon the aspects of teaching that have historically proven to be more effective than today's "experiments," while you embrace the modern methods that do work today. I hope you have principals who believe in firm discipline, because otherwise, your students won't learn very much. And finally, I hope you are filled with a great amount of dedication as you set forth to mold and enrich our future

American decision makers.

In spite of what I have stated about the importance of the classroom educator possessing extensive knowledge of subject matter, it is vitally important that you, yourself, want to learn more. There are some who say that teaching is learning, and that is true. There is always deeper knowledge to learn from any subject, and it is fun and agreeable to discover new knowledge with your students. It's the working together to gather new information that bonds a teacher with her students, and the students with their teacher. So don't be afraid to say, "I don't know. Let's find out together." It's fun! Also, the most imperative aspect of effective teaching is dedication and caring desire for students to excel scholastically, and the ability to convey information in a clear, comprehensive fashion, which in turn should result in student ease of understanding. A teacher's expectancy of optimum effort on the part of students is imperative. No one ever said that school is easy. Life in general, is not usually easy. The idea that hard work and sustained effort should not be expected of children has had a detrimental effect on young people of today. I believe this perfidious rationale that has been transmitted to our young people in so many ways, has led to the high suicide rate among teenagers in recent years. After having been told that effort is not necessary to succeed in life, many youths are finding the many real life challenges just too overwhelming. Children must learn from early on, that there is very little to be attained in this world without the utilization of hard work and effort, for as Arthur Brisbane quips: "The dictionary is the only place where success comes before work." We would all do well to advise our children of this sound logic.

Our world is a pretty wonderful place, and we have vast opportunities, especially in America, to live useful, fulfilling, fruitful lives filled with peace and joy, but it generally is not without some struggle, some challenge. To tell our children that the world is always fair, always easy, is doing them a dire disservice. The youth of America deserves better than that.

The deciding factor in our country's ability to maintain the status of a first rate, first world nation is QUALITY and EQUALITY in education. It is the duty of every American to play an active role in securing our prominence in the world. Total reformation cannot be achieved overnight, but certain positive steps can be taken in our homes, in our schools, and in our legal system to restore accountability to American life. Misinformation, erroneous expectations, and complacency in our homes and in our schools can no longer be tolerated. Now is the time for relevant reflection and profound thought, for it is true that "evil begins when good men do nothing."

It is of vital interest to our quality of life, and to our hope for the future, to ensure that quality education serves our nation's youth. This must be considered a national priority for the spiritual and intellectual health of this country's future--- our American children.

CHILDREN FIRST CREDO

I believe in children's laughter, the sweet perfume of a newborn baby's skin, and that every child is entitled to happiness, decent housing, health care, proper nutrition, and a good education.

I believe that our schools should be places of discovery and growth, not of danger; that teachers should be paid more than lawyers, and that parenting should be a required course in every high school.

I believe that "quality time" is a phony notion that cannot substitute for substantial time spent with our children. I believe that baseball and other children's games can be magical, and should be "wrested" from screaming, competitive coaches and parents and return to play. I believe that childhood should be a time of sandcastles and celebration, and that the defense of innocence is as important as our borders.

I believe that our most urgent mission should be putting the needs of our children first.

By Jane Daugherty, Children First Editor
Detroit Free Press - 1995

8th GRADE FINAL EXAM

Grammar (Time, one hour)

1. Give nine rules for the use of Capital Letters.

2. Name the Parts of Speech and define those that have no Modifications.

3. Define Verse, Stanza and Paragraph.

4. What are the Principal Parts of a verb? Give Principal Parts of lie, lay and run

5. Define Case.. Illustrate each Case.

6. What is Punctuation? Give rules for principal marks of Punctuation.

7. Write a composition of about 150 words and show therein that you understand the practical use of the rules of grammar.

Arithmetic (Time, 1.25 hours)

1. Name and define the Fundamental Rules of Arithmetic.

2. A wagon box is 2 ft deep, 10 feet long, and 3 ft. wide. How many bushels of wheat will it hold?

3. If a load of wheat weighs 3942 lbs., what is it worth at 50cts/bushel, deducting 1050lbs. for tare?

4. District No. 33 has a valuation of $35,000. What is the necessary levy to carry on a school seven months at $50 per month, and have $104 for incidentals?

5. Find cost of 6720 lbs. coal at $6.00 per ton.

6. Find the interest of $512.60 for 8 months and 18 days at 7 percent.

7. What is the cost of 40 boards 12 inches wide and 16

ft. long at $20 per meter?

8. Find bank discount on $300 for 90 days (no grace) at 10 percent.

9. What is the cost of a square farm at $15 per acre, the distance around which is 640 rods?

10. Write a Bank Check, a Promissory Note, and a Receipt.

U. S. History (Time, 45 minutes)

1. Give the epochs into which U. S. History is divided.

2. Give an account of the discovery of America by Columbus.

3. Relate the causes and results of the Revolutionary War.

4. Show the territorial growth of the United States.

5. Tell what you can of the history of Kansas.

6. Describe three of the most prominent battles of the Rebellion.

7. Who were the following: Morse, Whitney, Fulton, Bell, Lincoln, Penn, and Howe?

8. Name events connected with the following dates: 1607, 1620, 1800, 1849, 1865.

Orthography (Time, one hour)

1. What is meant by the following: Alphabet, phonetic, orthography, etymology, syllabication?

2. What are elementary sounds? How classified?

3. What are the following, and give examples of each: Trigraph, sub vocals, diphthong, cognate letters, linguals?

4. Give four substitutes for caret 'u'.

5. Give two rules for spelling words with final 'e.' Name two exceptions under each rule. 6. Give two uses of silent letters in spelling. Illustrate each.

7. Define the following prefixes and use in connection with a word: bi, dis, mis, pre, semi, post, non, inter, mono, sup.

8. Mark diacritically and divide into syllables the following, and name the sign that indicates the sound: card, ball, mercy, sir, odd, cell, rise, blood, fare, last.

9. Use the following correctly in sentences: cite, site, sight, fane, fain, feign, vane, vain, vein, raze, raise, rays.

10. Write 10 words frequently mispronounced and indicate pronunciation by use of diacritical marks and by syllabication.

Geography (Time, one hour)

1. What is climate? Upon what does climate depend?

2. How do you account for the extremes of climate in Kansas?

3. Of what use are rivers? Of what use is the ocean?

4. Describe the mountains of North America.

5. Name and describe the following: Monrovia, Odessa, Denver, Manitoba, Hecla, Yukon, St. Helena, Juan Fernandez, Aspinwall & Orinoco.

6. Name and locate the principal trade centers of the U.S.

7. Name all the republics of Europe and give the capital of each.

8. Why is the Atlantic Coast colder than the Pacific in the same latitude?

9. Describe the process by which the water of the ocean

returns to the sources of rivers.

10. Describe the movements of the earth. Give the inclination of the earth. [30]

NOTES

1. Edward A. Wynne, EDUCATION WEEK, November 15, 1989.

2. John Silber, STRAIGHT SHOOTING: WHAT'S WRONG WITH AMERICA AND HOW TO FIX IT, 1989.

3. Ibid.

4. "Our Opinion, Editorial, "A Stinging Indictment", THE DETROIT NEWS, 1990.

5. William Raspberry, Editorial, "Culture and Education in America", THE DETROIT NEWS, 1990.

6. Chauncey Bailey, "PARENTS, SCHOOLS ARE FAILING OUR KIDS", THE DETROIT NEWS, 1990.

7. Mark Hornbeck, (Lansing News Bureau), "The Money Myth, THE DETROIT NEWS, June 11, 1989.

8. Dr. John Bowlby, Lecture, October, 1990, Northville, Michigan.

9. THE DETROIT NEWS, April 24, 1995.

10. George Cantor, "Today's Students – The Losers in the Education War? ", THE DETROIT NEWS, 1990.

11. Gregory R. Anrig and Archie E. LaPoint, EDUCATION LEADERSHIP, Vol.47, November 1989.

12. George Will, "Real Education Needs Real Work", THE DETROIT NEWS, 1990.

13. George Will, "Real Education Needs Real Work" THE DETROIT NEWS, 1989.

14. Richard E. Burr, "Are Today's Youngsters Really Better Educated?" THE DETROIT NEWS, 1990.

15. George Will, "The Yellow Peril on Campus", THE DETROIT NEWS, 1990.

16. Warren T. Brooks, "Information Revolution Could Bury Us", Source: Arthur D. Little, Inc., THE DETROIT NEWS.

17. STATISTICAL ABSTRACT OF THE UNITED STATES, The National Data Book – U.S. department of Commerce, Bureau

of Census, Barbara Everitt-Bryant, Director.

18. John J. Dilulio, "Crime in America: It's Going to Get Worse", <u>READER'S DIGEST</u>, August, 1995.

19. Gerald Greenwald, Speech at National Association of Black Automotive Suppliers Scholarly Dinner, excerpted by THE DETROIT NEWS, 1990.

20. "Dear Abby", THE DETROIT NEWS.

21. Laura Sessions, WASHINGTON POST, excerpted by <u>READER'S DIGEST</u>, August, 1995.

22. Patricia Summerside, "South Dakota Schools; More than Money Can buy", adapted from <u>WINTER POLICY REVIEW</u>, 1990.

23. Jesse Jackson, "Attitudes, Not Aptitude, Determines Altitude", THE DETROIT NEWS, 1990.

24. "Dear Abby", "U.S. Students Learn Sad Lesson to Grades", THE DETROIT NEWS, 1991.

25. John W. Wright, <u>THE UNIVERSAL ALMANAC</u>, Universal Press, 1990.

26. Thomas Sowell, "Closed Minds Dominate Most Campuses", THE DETROIT NEWS, 1990.

27. "Postscript", THE DETROIT NEWS, 1990.

<u>28. EDUCATION WEEK</u>, November, 1989.

29. Ibid.

30. Smokey Valley Genealogy Society Collection. Salina, KA (source from 1895).

LaVergne, TN USA
06 September 2010
196059LV00003B/18/P